ASIAPAC BOOKS

Inspiration from
Confucius

— Choice Quotations from the Analects —

Compiled by Chen Wangheng
Illustrated by Jeffrey Seow

ASIAPAC • SINGAPORE

Publisher
ASIAPAC BOOKS PTE LTD
996 Bendemeer Road #06-09
Singapore 339944
Tel: (65) 6392 8455
Fax: (65) 6392 6455
Email: asiapacbooks@pacific.net.sg

Come visit us at our Internet home page
www.asiapacbooks.com

First published January 2006
4th edition July 2008

ISBN 13 978-981-229-398-5
ISBN 10 981-229-398-1

Inspiration/reflection by Lim SK
Translation by Yang Liping (inspiration/reflection)
Cover illustrations by Jeffrey Seow
Cover design by Wing Fee
Page layout by Kelly Lim
Body text in 9pt Helvetica
Edited by Sin Yoke Yin
Printed in Singapore by FuIsland Offset Printing

Publisher's Note

Confucius is indeed a great sage who has left behind a legacy of works that continues to impact every aspect of life in the modern age. Therefore it is with great pleasure that Asiapac brings to you this new edition of *Inspiration from Confucius*.

Unlike most other philosophical works which have a didactic tone, *The Analects* conveys the tenets of Confucius' teachings by describing the actions of the sage in his daily life. *The Analects*, compiled by Confucius' disciples who each saw their master from a different perspective, offers a complete picture of the person of Confucius. For this reason, the Confucius we see in this book is affable yet stern, profound yet down to earth. This dismisses the stiff and stuffy images that many associate with the benign sage.

You will enjoy a broad coverage in this title:

1. A profile of Confucius, covering his life, career, teachings and influence.
2. Analysis of the *Analects*, including keywords used in the classic.
3. Best selections of the *Analects*, with inspirational thoughts.
4. An index of this selection, based on eight themes.
5. Reflections based on the *Analects* for the reader's application.

We would like to take this opportunity to thank Jeffrey Seow for his vivid drawings, Professor Chen Wangheng for his compilation and foreword, and the production team for their contribution to the publication of this book.

About the Compiler

Chen Wangheng, born in October 1944, is a professor in the Philosophy Department of Wuhan University in Hubei Province.

He is also a member of the executive council of the China National Society of Aesthetics, vice-president and secretary-general of the Hubei Provincial Society of Aesthetics, member of the International Society of Aesthetics, and foreign member of the American Society of Aesthetics. He is listed in various editions of *International Who's Who*, compiled by the Cambridge International Biography Centre of the United Kingdom and the American Biography Research Institute. Chen's landmark book *Chinese Bronzes: Ferocious Beauty* is published by Asiapac Books.

About the Illustrator

Jeffrey Seow 萧承财, a Singaporean artist, was born in 1954. A number of his works are imbued with a deep sense of morality. This stems from his own belief that life should be ordered around the practice of values. In *Inspiration from Confucius* and *Popular Chinese Idioms*, he has demonstrated his practical appreciation of traditional Chinese values. In his other works, *Legends of the Fortune Gods, Legends of the Gods of Wealth,* and *Legend of the Laughing Buddha*, he has successfully captured the images of the gods and brought much reading pleasure to our readers.

Foreword

Confucius is the No. One Chinese sage and Confucianism that he founded forms the mainstay of Chinese cultural tradition. Confucian culture has remained China's national foundation, providing the fundamental moral principles for conduct for the Chinese people over the past thousands of years.

Confucius has not left behind any independent works. The main ideas that he espoused and we know today are contained in the *Analects of Confucius*. Confucius's thoughts can well be summed up by the following terms taken from the *Great Learning*: heart rectification, moral cultivation, family regulation, state governing and bringing peace to the land. Rectifying one's heart and cultivating one's moral integrity are both matters of personal cultivation. State governing and bringing peace to the land pertain to state administration. Family regulation involves ways of managing one's family. Confucianism emphasizes family management because a family is deemed to be just like a state and they are managed in roughly the same way. A good family manager will naturally make a successful state ruler. Family management consists mainly in handling the ethical relationship between father and children as well as that between brothers. To handle well these two relationships, one should abide by two basic moral principles: filial piety towards one's parents and respect towards one's brothers. Only thus can family management advance smoothly towards state administration, filial piety progress into loyalty, and brotherly respect expand into justice.

Love underlies filial piety and brotherly respect. The final purpose of moral cultivation is to develop human love. The core concept of Confucianism—*ren* (humanity or benevolence)—is actually based on love. "Fan Chi asked what benevolence was. Confucius said, 'Love your fellow men.'" Domestic harmony will be achieved when a family is regulated by love; national unity will be attained when a state is ruled by love; international peace will be obtained when the world is governed by love. Confucius does not advocate an unprincipled love. Here two principles come into play. First, "a benevolent man helps others to take their stand in so far as he himself wishes to take his stand, and gets others there in so far as he himself wishes to get there." Second, "do not impose what you do not want on others". Both principles govern the way of heart rectification.

Rectifying one's heart and engaging in moral cultivation are the foundation of the three major components of Confucianism, the other two being family regulation, state administration and bringing peace to the land.

Confucius thinks that a man is not born knowing everything and he grows to know the world through studying. Therefore, it is very important to study. Confucius was committed to education and came up with a series of valuable educational principles.

Self-consciousness and self-examination are emphasized as far as personal cultivation is concerned. Confucius' student Zeng Zi said, "I examine myself everyday on the following three matters: Have I done my best in planning matters for others? Have I kept faithful to my friends? Have I thought over what I teach to others?"

Confucian scholars do not think it is a burden to rectify their hearts and cultivate their moral integrity. Rather they turn these tasks into an internal pursuit that is enjoyable spiritually as it integrates truth and turn everything for good. In essence, these tasks end up an aesthetic joy. That is also why Confucius says, "Is it not a pleasant thing to put into practice what you have learned from time to time? Is it not a joy to have friends come from afar? Is it not a gentlemanly manner not to take offence when your talents are not recognized by others?"

It is a delight to study and make friends. Study is a delight because it can improve our moral integrity; friendship delights us because it expands our external energy; not being angry with others who fail to appreciate our abilities demonstrates our lofty spiritual realm.

Confucius is a mountain looming high above the clouds in the history of human civilization.

Analects of Confucius is a treasured classic with its inexhaustible meanings that inspire wisdom and goodness.

Professor Chen Wangheng
Wuhan University
Hubei, China

Contents

Guide to Reading

Inspiration from Confucius contains best selections of 160 excerpts, based on these 10 concepts:

1. 仁 Benevolence/Humanity
2. 义 Justice
3. 礼 Propriety/Rites
4. 知 Knowing
5. 信 Trust
6. 忠 Loyalty
7. 孝 Filial Piety
8. 正 Correctness, Propriety, Legality or Rectifying
9. 学 Study
10. 行 Action and Practice or Conduct

Page format:

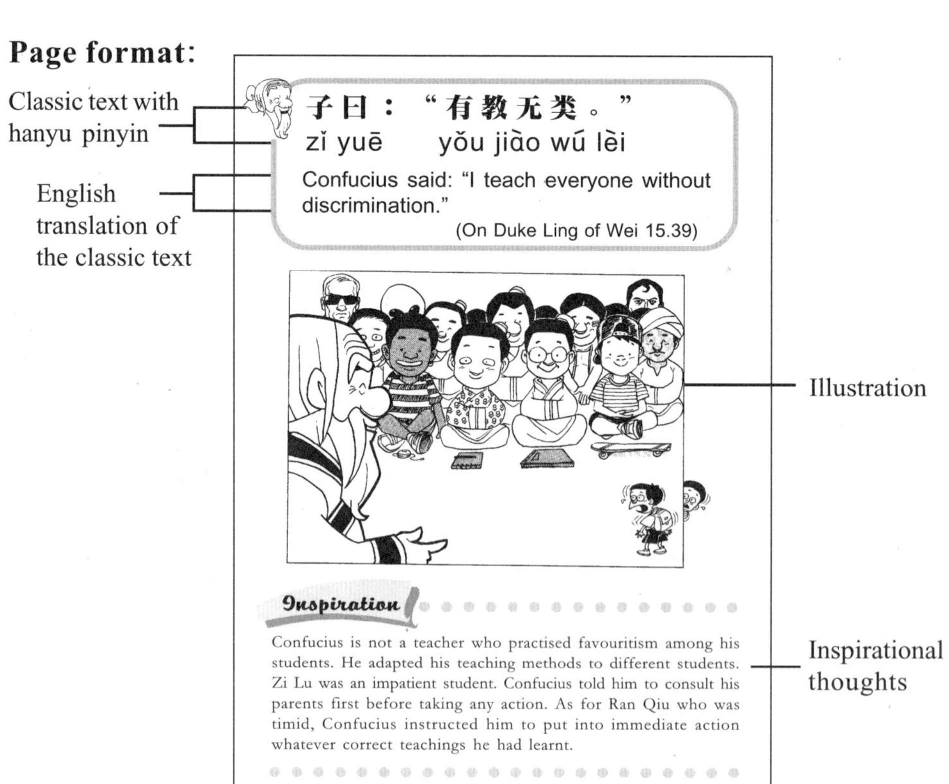

Profile of Confucius

Original name	:	Kong Qiu, with the literary name of Zhongni.
Date of birth	:	August 27, 551 BC
Date of death	:	February 11, 479 BC
Native place	:	Zouyi, Changping Township, State of Lu (now Qufu County, Shandong Province)
Family members	:	Father: Shu Liang He Mother: Yan Zheng Zai One brother and nine sisters Wife: Qi Guan of Song Son: Kong Li
Academic attainments	:	Studied at the village school in childhood, taught himself at 15 and read the *Book of Songs* and the *Book of History*.
Hobbies	:	Study, teaching, playing zither, singing and reading poetry.
Idol	:	Duke Zhou

Confucius' Life

Birth

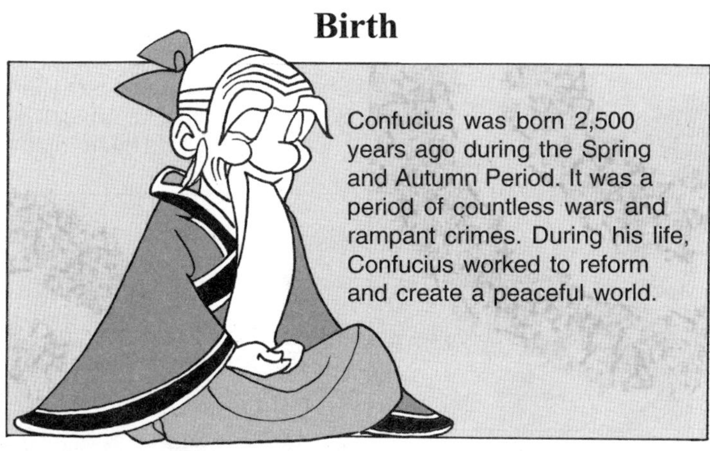

Confucius' father, Shu Liang He, was a knight from a corner county in Lu. His first wife gave birth to nine daughters!

Shu Liang He, who was over 60, married young Yan Zheng Zai. The couple made several trips to Mt. Niqiu to pray for a son. Not long after, Yan Zheng Zai conceived. Confucius was born in Mt. Niqiu. To commemorate Confucius' birth at Mt. Niqiu, he was called Kong Qiu, alias Zhong Ni*.

** Brothers were often named Bo, Zhong, Shu and Ji according to seniority. Being Shu Liang He's second son, Confucius was named Zhong Ni. His elder brother was named Bo Ni.*

Early Years

Shu Liang He passed away in 549 BC when Confucius was only three. He was brought up by his mother.

Yan Zheng Zai encouraged her son to learn and sent him to school.

Confucius was very interested in rites and rituals since young. He liked to observe the rites held at the ancestral temple in Qu Fu (the capital city of Lu). On returning home, he would mimic these rites.

When he was 17, Confucius' mother passed away. Confucius buried his mother with his father. At 19, Confucius got married. His wife was Qi Guan. One year later, a son was born. Confucius was very happy, therefore he named his son Kong Li (carp), alias Bo Yu.

Learning

Not bad. You may now learn a new tune.
I'm still not used to the beat yet. Please let me continue.
Confucius was very keen and serious in his learning. Besides self-study, he learned music from Shi Xiang, Lao Zi and Chang Hong.
Another 10 days...
I still cannot express the meaning of the tune. Please let me go on.
Well, if you insist...
Again, another 10 days flew by...
Wonderful playing! How enchanting!
You have truly mastered this piece of music.
Yes, I can sense the rich feelings and high aspirations expressed in this tune. It is most exquisite!

Education and Teaching

When Confucius was 30, he built a platform under a big apricot tree in his yard and began to take in pupils to pass on his learning.

Confucius is setting up a school!

His fees must be very high.

Not at all, only 10 pieces of dried meat will suffice, and he will take anyone regardless of status or age.

Confucius accepted all kinds of people as his students, as many as over 3,000. Seventy-two of them proved to be outstanding men. In the past, culture and education were privileges enjoyed only by the aristocrats. Confucius broke this tradition when he set up a private school and provided education for the common people. He was China's first great educator.

The 10 Most Outstanding Disciples of Confucius

Yan Hui (Zi Yuan)

Zhong You (Zi Lu)

Duanmu Ci (Zi Gong)

Min Sun (Zi Qian)

Ran Geng (Bo Niu)

Ran Yong (Zhong Gong)

Ran Qiu (Zi You)

Zai Yu (Zi Wo)

Yan Yan (Zi You)

Bu Shang (Zi Xia)

Official Career

As Minister of Justice, Confucius was responsible for security, enforcement of law and punishment. After he assumed office, criminal offences were greatly reduced and there was also obvious improvement in social security.

Tour of the Various States

A learned man may also have lofty ideals but these are not necessarily well-received by men.

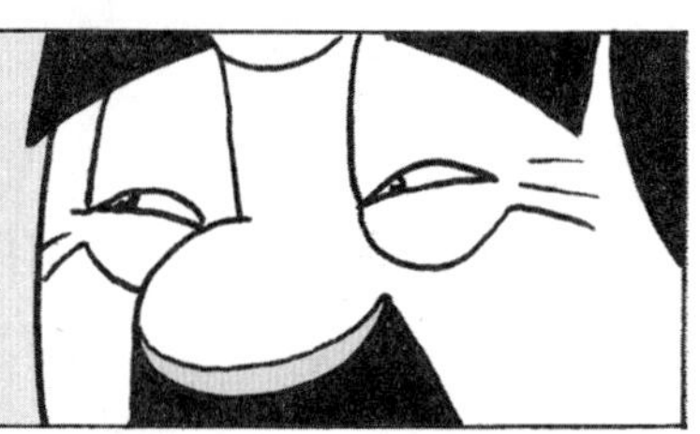

For 14 years, Confucius toured the various states, hoping for an opportunity to show his ability in governance and realize his political ideals. Unfortunately, none of the princes and aristocrats in the various states would use him. Fourteen years had passed and Confucius was already 68! On the road home, Confucius reflected on the years that had gone by:

Wind in the valley, foggy and rainy
Returning son, far in the wilds
Other than the sky, no place for him
Roaming the world, no fixed abode
Men in darkness hiding, virtue unknown
But the years lengthen, old age comes

Old Age

Upon his return to Lu, he became advisor to the Duke of Lu, continued teaching and edited the *Book of Songs* and the *Spring and Autumn Annals (Chun Qiu).* In his writing, he was concerned with "knowing one's place in society". Rebellious acts involving sons murdering fathers or ministers murdering their lords were criticised. His stance and sense of what's right and wrong were made clear. The *Annals* has been said to have made "rebellious ministers and wicked men fearful".

In 479 BC, Confucius passed away. He was 73. Confucius was buried north of Qu Fu on the banks of the Zhu River. His disciples mourned for him and could not bear to leave his grave. Some even kept watch over it for six years. During the period of mourning, they recorded what he had said and done in his life. This record has been passed down to us as the *Analects*.

Confucius' Achievements and Influence

Confucianism became the only doctrine advocated during the reign of Emperor Wu of Han. As a result, Confucianism evolved into an orthodox thought which had dominated Chinese society for some 2,000 years. Study of Confucian classics was also elevated as a required pathway leading to the official world. There had also been a highly customary practice among the civilians to offer sacrifice to Confucius. Uncountable Confucian temples were built across China. Children used to pay their tribute to Confucius first before starting their school education.

Since Emperor Gaozu of Han took the lead in offering sacrifice to Confucius in the 12th month of 195 BC according to the lunar calendar, emperors of different periods, such as Emperor Xiaowen of Northern Wei, Emperors Gaozong and Xuanzong of Tang, Emperor Zhenzong of Song, Emperors Kangxi and Qianlong of Qing, had all paid personal visits to Qufu, Confucius' hometown, to show their respects.

Chinese emperors had also granted many posthumous titles to Confucius. For example, Emperor Xiaowen of Northern Wei granted him the title of "Father Zhongni, the Literary Sage", Emperor Wen of Sui "Our Late Father Mentor", Emperor Taizong of Tang "Our Late Sage", Emperor Xuanzong of Tang "King of Literary Minds", Emperor Shizong of Ming and Emperor Shizu of Qing "Our Late Mentor who reached sainthood".

Important Events in the Life of Confucius

Year	Age	Important Events
551 BC	Born in Lu	village of Qu Fu in Shandong
549 BC	3	father Shu Liang He passed away
537 BC	15	decided to pursue learning
535 BC	17	mother Yan Zheng Zai passed away
533 BC	19	married Qi Guan
532 BC	20	birth of son Kong Li; made manager of state granaries
531 BC	21	made overseer of flocks and grazing grounds of Lu
523 BC	29	visited Luoyang to investigate the origin of ritual and music; consulted Lao Zi about ritual and Chang Hong about music
522 BC	30	established in the six skills; began to take in pupils
517 BC	35	the three *Hengs* united their armies and attacked Duke Zhao, who fled to Qi
515 BC	37	aristocrats of Qi plotted to kill Confucius; Confucius decided to return to Lu
505 BC	47	Yang Hu rebelled; Yang Hu tried to get Confucius' help but Confucius declined
501 BC	51	appointed governor of the middle district of Lu
500 BC	52	promoted to Minister of Justice, and later Premier; accompanied his king to Qi for a conference at Jia Valley and clinched diplomatic victory there
498 BC	54	persuaded Duke Ding to tear down the fortresses of the three *Hengs*; though this was not completely successful, the power of the three *Hengs* was visibly diminished
497 BC	55	left Lu and began his tour of the states; first stop was Wei; left Wei for Chen; passing through the city of Kuang, the party was trapped by the Kuang men
493 BC	59	arrived at Song; Si Ma Heng Tui of Song wanted to kill him, so he fled to Zheng; arrived in Wei, Song
490 BC	62	arrived at Cai
489 BC	63	trapped between Chen and Cai; food supplies were cut off for seven days
484 BC	68	accepted the invitation of Ji Kang Zi and returned to Lu; concentrated on teaching and writing
483 BC	69	death of son Kong Li
481 BC	71	death of Yan Hui; the king of Lu shot a unicorn during a hunt
480 BC	72	death of Zi Lu during a revolt in Wei
479 BC	73	passing away of Confucius; buried north of Qu Fu beside the Zhu River

Introduction to the *Analects*

Lun-yu (The *Analects*) is a record of the life and sayings of the renowned Chinese thinker Confucius. Consisting of 20 chapters and 492 sections, the book was compiled by Confucius's disciples after Confucius's death. These chapters and sections are not arranged in any fixed order.

The Core Concepts of the *Analects*

Confucius' thoughts are centred on the concept of "benevolence/humanity".

1. Political ideas: Ruling by virtue, instructing and regulating the people through education and rites/propriety; the rulers need to be upright in words and deeds and know how to promote upright men so as to win the popular trust.
2. Educational ideas: Non-discriminatory policies are to be followed in education, guaranteeing education for everyone; teaching methods and educational content need to be adapted to differing students and emphasis placed on respecting diverse personalities.
3. Ethical ideas: Filial piety is the fundamental principle of benevolence, which can be extended to other virtues. Filial piety does not simply mean financial provision for one's parents. It also requires a sincere, respectful and grateful heart.
4. Ideas on material wealth: Confucius did not oppose material pursuit. Yet he maintained that wealth should be obtained in a legitimate way. Wealth acquired by illegitimate means is like fleeting clouds. A man of benevolence and morality can keep his mind undisturbed by either poverty or prosperity.

The "Ideal Personality" as seen in the *Analects*

Confucius portrayed for us an ideal personality in "the gentleman", in whom benevolence/humanity, justice and morality are concentrated. Pitted against this gentleman is "the petty man" of despicable moral qualities.

1. The gentleman seeks justice while the petty man pursues profit.
2. The gentleman is magnanimous while the petty man is always filled with anxieties.
3. The gentleman seeks unity rather than collusion while the petty man is bent on collusion instead of unity.
4. The gentleman helps others fulfil their goals while the petty man leads others astray.
5. The gentleman is strict with himself while the petty man is strict with others.
6. The gentleman is able to live with poverty and conform to the Way while the petty man acts impulsively against the law when in poverty.

The Value of the *Analects*

The *Analects*, the *Great Learning*, the *Doctrine of the Mean* and the *Book of Mencius* are collectively called the Four Books. They were required reading for Chinese children in the past. Confucius lived over 2,000 years ago, but many of the ideas and wisdom contained in the *Analects* remain valid today.

1. **Education for personality:** Many educational institutions have realised that mere delivery of knowledge does not constitute a sound education. Education for personality development is also very important. Confucius adopted a heuristic method of instruction to improve his students' ability to think independently by encouraging them to draw inferences about other cases from one instance. He also adjusted his teaching methods in the light of the students' diverse characters and levels of intelligence. He encouraged his students to think more, observe more, and study more. They were also required to keep watch over their own words and deeds and examine themselves so as to grow in benevolence.

2. **Guide to maintaining a sound self-community relationship:** Confucius attached great importance to the self's relationship with the community. Rulers, officials, parents and children are expected to faithfully perform their own duties. This is the basic condition for maintaining social order. People should treat each other with honesty and trust, and be considerate of each other. "What you do not want done to yourself, do not do to others." Only thus can a harmonious relationship be achieved between the self and the community, and social order maintained.

3. **Leadership training:** Modern society pays much attention to leadership training and there are numerous books exploring this subject. Actually, the *Analects* can be a workable guide on this. Confucius set forth the most basic quality to be expected of a leader, that is, a ruler needs to have "correct personal conduct". Confucius said: "When a prince's personal conduct is correct, his government is effective without the issuing of orders. If his personal conduct is not correct, he may issue orders, but they will not be followed." A ruler cannot convince others unless he sets himself as an example.

4. **The way for managing state affairs and bringing peace to the people:** According to Confucius, popular trust is the pillar of state administration. A state cannot be well managed without popular trust. Before the state can be effectively managed, help the people to become wealthy and then educate them. These principles for state administration still remain valid today.

Keywords of the *Analects*

Ren (Benevolence/Humanity)

The Chinese character for benevolence (仁) consists of a left "人 (*ren*, man)" and a right "二 (*er*, two), meaning the relationship between two men. Now, it refers to interpersonal care and love in general.

Benevolence has a multiplicity of meanings, such as:

1. Love of human beings: interpersonal respect and love
2. Self-denial and return to propriety: restraining oneself and acting in conformity with the propriety/rites
3. Loyalty and benevolence: being considerate and not imposing what you don't want on others
4. Five virtues: gravity, generosity of soul, sincerity, earnestness, and kindness

Yi (Justice)

On Virtue 4.16: The gentleman considers righteousness; the petty man...
On Zi Zhang19.1: A learned man, in the face of danger, is willing to lay...
On Duke Ling of Wei 15.18: When one abides by righteousness as a...
On Transmitting 7.16: Ill-gotten riches are to me just as clouds passing...

The complex Chinese character for justice (義) is made up of an upper "羊(*yang*, sheep)" and a lower "我(*wo*, I)." In the lower portion, a hand is seen holding a dagger. Thus, the character implies that a gentle sheep can overcome the aggressive "I". This also explains its meaning: personal interests come after moral principles.

Confucius believed that a gentleman should take justice as the fundamental principle. It is a sign of a lack of courage if justice is recognized and yet not upheld and promoted. Wealth and status is what everybody desires. However, they should be first measured by the standard of justice. Wealth and status acquired in an illegitimate manner are worth nothing.

Li (Propriety/Rites)

On Yan Yuan 12.1: To be able to overcome your desire and observe the...
On Yan Yuan 12.5: If a gentleman is excellent in his work, does nothing...
On Tai Bo 8.8: The Book of Songs inspires me, the rites provide me with...
On Tai Bo 8.2: Courtesy without following the rites leads to weariness...

The complex Chinese character for propriety (禮) is thus structured: two pieces of jadestone (*yu*, 玉) are placed in a ritual container (*dou*, 豆). It means solemn ceremonies are conducted to pray for heavenly blessings. From this, many other meanings such as respectful, polite, and rituals are derived. In ancient time, propriety was a very important branch of learning, a part of the six arts: propriety (rites), music, archery, chariot-riding, calligraphy and arithmetic.

Propriety does not refer to superficial regulations like etiquette. Confucius considered propriety as both the rules and the purpose for performing benevolent actions. Self-denial and return to propriety are done for the sake of benevolence. Don't look at, listen to, talk about or do what goes against propriety. Thus, the world will return to the state of benevolence.

***Zhi* (Knowing)**

> On Governing 2.17: If you understand, say that you understand. If you do...
> About Yong Ye 6.20: Those who have knowledge cannot be compared...
> On Transmitting 7.20: I was not born with knowledge. It's just that I have...
> On Yan Yuan 12.22: Fan Chi asked further: "What is wisdom?"...
> On Learning 1.16: Do not worry about not being understood but be...

Knowing means "being conscious of" or "obtaining the knowledge of". In the *Analects*, knowing can also mean "intellect (wisdom)", such as "A man of wisdom will not be cheated." and "A wise man knows how to gain the benefits of virtue." In fact, these two meanings are closely related. Confucius said: "When you know something, admit that you know it; and when you do not know something, admit that you do not know it; this is knowledge."

Knowing a person is an important part of this "knowing". Confucius believed that a person does not need to worry if he is understood by others; he needs only to worry if he understands others. Knowing a person is of particular importance to leaders and administrators. Only if a leader or administrator knows others can he recognize and promote the talents. How does a person know others? For Confucius, a person should not rush to a conclusion about a popular person before conducting a careful investigation. He is supposed to listen to what another person says and observe what he does in order to see if he can match his actions to his words.

***Xin* (Trust)**

On Transmitting 7.25: Confucius educated his students in four disciplines...
On Yan Yuan 12.7: Without the people's trust, the government cannot...
On Governing 2.22: If a person is not trustworthy, how can he establish...
The Master Seldom 9.25: Vaule loyalty and trustworthiness above all...
On Gong Ye Zhang 5.26: I hope to see the aged enjoy peace, there is...

The Chinese character for trust (信) consists of two parts: 人 (*ren*, human being) and 言 (*yan*, speech). A person cannot establish trust and creditability if he does not honour his words and match his words with action.

Confucius placed a great emphasis on the virtue of trust. He did not think that a person without trust can secure a foothold in society. This is no different from a large carriage without the crossbar to yoke an ox or a small carriage without the crossbar to harness a horse. How can such carriages be made to move? An honest person who honours his words can get along with people wherever he goes.

Confucius said: "He acts before he speaks, and afterwards speaks according to his action." A person will lose the trust of others if he fails to act on his words or overstates the facts. This is what a gentleman hates. He who boasts with no sense of shame will find it difficult to put into practice what he says. Therefore, a person should be cautious about and responsible for his words because this is a way to win trust.

In politics, Confucius also stressed the importance of popular trust. Under special circumstances, the government may give up its military facilities or food supplies. However, popular trust is something that a government cannot afford to lose. Without this support, a state will not last long despite its considerable strength.

Zhong (Loyalty)

On Learning 1.4: Zeng Zi said: "Daily, I examine myself in three areas...
On Transmitting 7.25: Confucius educated his students in four...
On Yan Yuan 12.23: Zi Gong asked about friendship...
Xian Questions 14.7: Confucius said: "If you love a person, how can you...
The Chief of the Ji Family 16.10: There are nine things which a...

Graphically, the Chinese character for loyalty (忠) has an upper part shaped like an arrow lodged in the target centre. The lower part stands for "heart." Therefore, *zhong* represents a sincere and fair heart.

Confucius instructed his students from the following four perspectives: classics, practice, loyalty and trust. He emphasized that our personal conduct should be guided by the principles of loyalty and trust.

We should do our best for others, especially our superiors and leaders. Loyalty stems from sincerity. We need to speak frankly when necessary. No selfish concerns, no fears.

Being faithful or loyal to somebody does not mean we have to comply with his wishes in everything. If necessary, we may also need to instruct and advise him. However, honest words do not sound pleasant. If he refuses our advice, do not insist. Otherwise, we will get ourselves into trouble.

Xiao (Filial Piety)

On Learning 1.2:	A man who is filial to his parents and respects his elder brothers is seldom disposed to rebel against the...
On Learning 1.11:	When a man's father is alive, check his aspirations. When a man's father is deceased, observe his...
On Governing 2.7:	These days, meeting the physical needs of parents is considered filial piety. But even dogs and horses are...

Filial piety is one of the basic moral principles. He who takes care of his parents and respect his elder brothers hardly does anything insubordinate. Can we expect an undutiful man to be honest with his friends or be loyal to the king?

Filial piety does not merely mean taking care of one's parents. One is also expected to look after one's dogs and horses at home. Without heartfelt respect towards one's parents, what is the difference between taking care of one's parents and feeding the animals?

The filial piety that Confucius advocated is never an unreasonable piety. If one's parents make a mistake, one should point it out in a restrained manner. If the parents do not admit it, one should continue to respect them rather than harbour any resentment.

Zheng (Correctness, Propriety, Legality or Rectifying)

On Yan Yuan 12.17: To govern means to be upright. If you lead the people...
On Zi Lu 13.6: If the ruler is upright, even if he does not issue orders...
On Zi Lu 13.3: Without establishing proper titles, one's instructions...
When in the Village 10.12: If the sitting mat is not laid according to the...
When in the Village 10.26: Before boarding the carriage, stand upright...

In the *Analects*, *zheng* has another layer of meaning—government. "To govern a state means to correct." When the rulers govern the state and people with the "correct Way", who dares to adhere to the incorrect way? To rectify others, one needs to be correct first. If one is correct, one does not need to issue orders. Otherwise, orders issued will not be obeyed. This is exactly what the following Chinese idiom means: "When the upper beam is not straight, the lower one will also go aslant." If those in senior positions set a good example of being upright and honest, those in subordinate positions will follow suit instead of comitting all kinds of outrages.

Social order cannot be maintained unless a "correct name" is established. "Let the ruler be a ruler, the subject a subject, the father a father, and the son a son." Each person should live and perform his duties appropriate to his role. "Without a correct name, your words do not sound reasonable. When your words are not reasonable, you cannot accomplish anything."

***Xue* (Study)**

On Learning 1.1: Isn't it a joy to acquire knowledge and be able to put it...
On Governing 2.15: Reading and studying without thinking is futile labour...
On Transmitting 7.2: Remembering the knowledge I have learnt, not...
On Tai Bo 8.17: Study as if time is not on your side. Learn as if you...
On Zi Zhang 19.13: Leisure time from official duty should be spent on...

Studying is not limited to books and ancient classics. Rather it also includes learning from other people. "When I am travelling with two men, I can surely find one of them worthy of being my teacher." We should learn from others' positive points and take their negative points as lessons. Thus, studying is actually present everywhere in our life.

How should we study? We need to keep our ears and eyes open, and work hard to broaden our vision. We also need to review what we have studied from time to time in order to obtain a better grasp of the acquired knowledge and gain new insights. In addition, it is important to combine studying and thinking. We will become confused if we do not think while studying. Similarly, it is useless to indulge in groundless contemplation.

Studying itself is a pleasant thing. However, that is not its final purpose. A man will remain a dumb bookworm who can merely recite the *Book of Songs* if he does not know how to put into practice what he learns.

Xing (Action and Practice or Conduct)

On Governing 2.13: He does not preach what he practises till he has...
On Virtue 4.24: A gentleman is slow to speak but prompt in action.
On Transmitting 7.25: Confucius educated his students in four...
On Transmitting 7.33: In terms of knowledge, I am quite accomplished...
On Duke Ling of Wei 15.18: When one abides by righteousness as a...

Xing is one of the four principles by which Confucius instructed his students, the other three being culture, loyalty and trust. By *Xing,* Confucius meant mainly moral cultivation such as filial piety towards one's parents, respect towards one's elder brothers, and honesty with one's friends. *Xing* comes before culture in Confucius' understanding: "If you have spare energy after attending to [moral] action, you may spend it making yourself cultured." Clearly he believed that moral conduct is more important than studying literature and arts.

Confucius stressed that one should match one's words with action or integrate knowledge with practice. To him, it is not enough to know a principle. It is important to put it into practice. He said: "Regarding moral principles, I do not know more than others. I need to do more in order to become a superior man in practice." Therefore, it is hard to comprehend a principle, yet it is even harder to practise it.

Best Selections of the *Analects*

DELIGHT OF STUDY

It is said that Confucius had over three thousand students and seventy-two of them stood out. He did not practise favouritism among his students in teaching, and was able to adapt his teaching methods to different students. He provided special instructions in the light of their diverse personalities . He also believed it was important to extract new insights from old knowledge and to ask others whenever any queries arose. A person needs to listen more, read more, and study more before he can become a learned man.

子曰："学而时习之，不亦说*乎？有朋自远方来，
zǐ yuē xué ér shí xí zhī bù yì yuè hū yǒu péng zì yuǎn fāng lái

不亦乐乎？人不知而不愠，不亦君子乎？"《学而1.1》
bù yì lè hū rén bù zhī ér bù yùn bù yì jūn zǐ hū

Confucius said: "Isn't it a joy to acquire knowledge and be able to put it to use? Isn't it a great pleasure to have a friend visiting from afar? Isn't he a gentleman who does not take offence at being slighted by others?"

(On Learning 1.1)

Inspiration

Confucius valued learning and not just the mere acquisition of knowledge. He believed that iron sharpens iron. Relating with friends can facilitate learning from each other.

*说：同"悦"。

子曰：“温故而知新，可以为师矣。” 《为政2.11》
zǐ yuē wēn gù ér zhī xīn kě yǐ wéi shī yǐ

Confucius said: “If one is able to learn new knowledge by reviewing old knowledge, he may then be a teacher of others.” (On Governing 2.11)

Inspiration

Confucius believed that learning should not just be a mere absorption of knowledge but to obtain new insights from old knowledge. In this way, real learning takes place.

子曰：“学而不思则罔*，思而不学则殆。”
zǐ yuē xué ér bù sī zé wǎng sī ér bù xué zé dài

《为政2.15》

Confucius said: "Reading and studying without thinking is futile labour. Thinking without reading and studying is perilous." (On Governing 2.15)

Inspiration

Learning involves two things: reading books and asking questions. We learn through raising quetions. By the same token, we should not let our minds be unrestrained or stick to one single aspect of thinking. Equal importance needs to be attached to both reading and thinking. This is the right attitude towards learning.

*罔：同“惘”。

子曰：“由，诲女* 知之乎？知之为知之，
zǐ yuē yóu huì rǔ zhī zhī hū zhī zhī wéi zhī zhī

不知为不知，是知也。” 《为政2.17》
bù zhī wéi bù zhī shì zhī yě

Confucius said: "Zhong You, do you understand what I'm saying? If you understand, say that you understand. If you do not understand, say that you do not understand. That is true knowledge indeed!" (On Governing 2.17)

Inspiration

The young Confucius would ask others whatever questions he had. Confucius said, "It conforms to the rites and rituals to ask when one doesn't understand!" True wisdom lies in one's confession about the limits of one's knowledge. The great Greek philosopher Socrates (470-399 BC) once remarked: "I only know one thing—that is I know nothing."

*女：同“汝”。

子曰：“知之者不如好之者，好之者不如乐之者。”
zǐ yuē zhī zhī zhě bù rú hào zhī zhě hào zhī zhě bù rú lè zhī zhě

《雍也6.20》

Confucius said: "Those who have knowledge cannot be compared with those who love knowledge. But even those who love knowledge cannot compare with those who delight in knowledge." (About Yong Ye 6.20)

Inspiration

Confucius once described himself as one who studied too hard to think of hunger, who was so happy that he put all worries behind him and even forgot he was growing old soon. If we do not have a true passion for learning, we can never reach such a stage.

子曰：“默而识* 之，学而不厌，诲人不倦，
zǐ yuē mò ér zhì zhī xué ér bù yàn huì rén bù juàn

何有于我哉？”《述而7. 2》
hé yǒu yú wǒ zāi

Confucius said: “Remembering the knowledge I have learnt, not feeling tired of learning and not growing weary in teaching—have I achieved all that?”
(On Transmitting 7.2)

Inspiration

Many people do not seek further education after graduation from schools or colleges. In fact, there is no end to studying and education is a lifelong effort. We may as well spend part of our spare time updating or expanding our existing knowledge so as to have a much more colourful life.

*识：“志”音，记住的意思。

子曰：“我非生而知之者，好古，敏以求之者也。”
zǐ yuē wǒ fēi shēng ér zhī zhī zhě hào gǔ mǐn yǐ qiú zhī zhě yě

《述而7.20》

Confucius said: “I was not born with knowledge. It’s just that I have a keen interest in ancient culture. So I pursue understanding with great diligence and an agile mind.” (On Transmitting 7.20)

Inspiration

Socrates had a similar saying: “I am not a wise man. But I love wisdom.” Whether you engage in academic study or other matters, you will not be able to persevere unless you are motivated by a strong interest or an earnest passion.

子曰：“三人行，必有我师焉。择其善者而
zǐ yuē sān rén xíng bì yǒu wǒ shī yān zé qí shàn zhě ér

从之，其不善者而改之。” 《述而7.22》
cóng zhī qí bú shàn zhě ér gǎi zhī

Confucius said: “Whenever I travel with others, there is always something I can learn from them. By observing them, I would pick out the virtues to emulate and the vices to check myself against.” (On Transmitting 7.22)

Inspiration

Confucius said, “When I am travelling with two men, I can surely find one of them worthy of being my teacher.” Who can be our teachers? Everybody has his or her strong and weak points. We can overcome our weak points by learning from others’ strong points and taking their weak points as warnings.

子曰：“盖有不知而作之者，我无是也。多闻，
zǐ yuē gài yǒu bù zhī ér zuò zhī zhě wǒ wú shì yě duō wén

择其善者而从之，多见而识*之，知之次也。”
zé qí shàn zhě ér cóng zhī duō jiàn ér zhì zhī zhī zhī cì yě

《述而7.28》

Confucius said: “I do not pretend to know what I do not know. I advocate listening to more opinions and selecting that which is good for learning. One must also be exposed to many things; this will broaden one's knowledge base. This way of learning is second perhaps only to a genius who knows everything.” (On Transmitting 7.28)

Inspiration

Widely respected as a mentor, Confucius never thought he knew everything. He was not born a genius. He became a man of profound learning through lifelong study and constant accumulation of knowledge. He took care to read more, listen more to others, and think more in his daily life.

*识：“志”音。

子与人歌而善，必使反之，而后和之。 《述而7.32》

zǐ yǔ rén gē ér shàn bì shǐ fǎn zhī ér hòu hè zhī

When anyone sang in the presence of Confucius a song that he liked, he never joined in at once but asked for it to be repeated and then joined in.

(On Transmitting 7.32)

Confucius was a learned man. But he did not become conceited because of this. He never let go of any opportunity to improve himself.

子曰：“学如不及，犹恐失之。” 《泰伯8.17》
zǐ yuē xué rú bù jí yóu kǒng shī zhī

Confucius said: “Study as if time is not on your side. Learn as if you may lose what you have acquired.” (On Tai Bo 8.17)

Inspiration

Acquired knowledge becomes unfamiliar if not used for a long time. Therefore, while mastering new knowledge, we need to review what we have studied regularly.

子曰：“性相近也，习相远也。” 《阳货17.2》
zǐ yuē xìng xiāng jìn yě xí xiāng yuǎn yě

Confucius said: "By nature, all men are alike. But differences in environment and practices make them turn out differently." (On Yang Huo 17.2)

Inspiration

The *Three-Character Classic* starts with "People at birth, / Are naturally good. // Their natures similar, / Yet habits different." The nature of man is like a piece of pure white silk thread in the beginning. It turns green when it is put in a vat of green dye. Men who grow up in different environments will develop divergent habits.

好仁不好学，其蔽也愚；好知*不好学，其蔽也荡；
hào rén bú hào xué qí bì yě yú hào zhì bú hào xué qí bì yě dàng

好信不好学，其蔽也贼；好直不好学，其蔽也绞；
hào xìn bú hào xué qí bì yě zéi hào zhí bú hào xué qí bì yě jiǎo

好勇不好学，其蔽也乱；好刚不好学，其蔽也狂。
hào yǒng bú hào xué qí bì yě luàn hào gāng bú hào xué qí bì yě kuáng

《阳货17.8》

Those who love benevolence but not learning may be easily fooled; those who love knowledge but not learning may lack self-control; those who love honesty but not learning may be taken advantage of; those who love frankness but not learning may hurt others with their rashness; those who love courage but not learning may cause chaos; those who love staunchness but not learning may be brash and reckless. (On Yang Huo 17.8)

Inspiration

Benevolence, knowledge, honesty, frankness, boldness (bellicosity) and staunchness are all virtues. Yet, if you just admire these virtues rather than try to practise them, it will not do you any good.

*知：智

子曰：“饱食终日，无所用心，难矣哉！
zǐ yuē bǎo shí zhōng rì wú suǒ yòng xīn nán yǐ zāi

不有博弈者乎？为之，犹贤乎已。”《阳货17.22》
bù yǒu bó yì zhě hū wéi zhī yóu xián hū yǐ

Confucius said: "A man who idles around after he has filled his stomach is good for nothing. Aren't there board games, one of which is chess? Even playing it is better than doing nothing." (On Yang Huo 17.22)

Inspiration

It is too wasteful to set your life goal on satisfying your hunger and nothing else. Do not let your heart and mind stay idle!

子夏曰："仕而优则学，学而优则仕。"
zì xià yuē shì ér yōu zé xué xué ér yōu zé shì

《子张19. 13》

Zi Xia said: "Leisure time from official duty should be spent on studies. Leisure time from studying should be spent on official duties." (On Zi Zhang 19.13)

Inspiration

Work and further education need to go hand-in-hand. Work can authenicate what is studied while proven learning can enhance work efficiency. They complement each other.

子曰：“自行束脩以上，吾未尝无诲焉！”
zǐ yuē zì xíng shù xiū yǐ shàng wú wèi cháng wú huì yān

《述而7.7》

Confucius said: "Whenever anyone wearing a *Shu Xiu** came to learn from me, I never rejected him." (On Transmitting 7.7)

Inspiration

Confucius is said to have more than three thousand students. Seventy-two of them stood out as his accomplished disciples. Confucius' students were of different origins, including nobles, ordinary people, merchants, politicians and warriors. Some of them were as old as Confucius while others were merely adolescents.

* *Shu Xiu refers to a head cloth worn by adolescents when they are about fifteen.*

子曰：“不愤不启，不悱不发；举一隅不以三
zǐ yuē bú fèn bù qǐ bù fěi bù fā jǔ yì yú bù yǐ sān

隅反，则不复也。” 《述而7.8》
yú fǎn zé bú fù yě

Confucius said: “Not until my students have struggled to the point of frustration with their questions and doubts will I enlighten them. Not until they have tussled intensely with wanting to say something but not knowing how to say it will I illuminate them. If for every principle I teach, they are not able to draw three other inferences, I will stop teaching them.” (On Transmitting 7.8)

Inspiration

The great Greek philosopher Socrates he would guide others to discover truth by themselves through dialogue, refutation and questioning. This is Isn't this quite similiar to Confucius's enlightening method in education?

子曰 ："二三子以我为隐乎？吾无隐乎尔！
zǐ yuē èr sān zǐ yǐ wǒ wéi yǐn hū wú wú yǐn hū ěr

吾无行而不与二三子者，是丘也。" 《述而7.24》
wú wú xíng ér bù yǔ èr sān zǐ zhě shì qiū yě

Confucius said to his students: "Do you suspect that I am holding back some of my knowledge from you? There is nothing I keep from you. This is what I, Kong Qiu, am like." (On Transmitting 7.24)

Inspiration

As an impartial mentor, Confucius instructed his son Kong Li in the same way he instructed his students.

子以四教：文，行，忠，信。 《述而7.25》
zǐ yǐ sì jiào wén xíng zhōng xìn

Confucius educated his students in four disciplines: culture, conduct, loyalty and good faith. (On Transmitting 7.25)

Inspiration

Students in ancient days were required to study "six arts": rites and rituals, music, archery, chariot-riding, calligraphy and arithmetic. Confucius taught a variety of courses. Far from being a fragile scholar, Confucius was actually an expert in archery and chariot-riding!

颜渊喟然叹曰：“仰之弥高，钻之弥坚，
yán yuān kuì rán tàn yuē yǎng zhī mí gāo zuān zhī mí jiān

瞻之在前，忽焉在后……” 《子罕9.11》
zhān zhī zài qián hū yān zài hòu

Yan Yuan said with a sigh: "The more I look up to master's teaching, the higher it seems. The more I dig into master's morals, the deeper it appears."
(The Master Seldom 9.11)

Inspiration

Yan Yuan worshipped Confucius as his idol and made considerable progress in learning by following his mentor. Actually, everybody has his or her idol or mentor. What is important here is whether this mentor is worthy of emulating or not, and whether he can motivate you to strive for constant advancement in your life and career.

子曰："有教无类。" 《卫灵公15.39》
zǐ yuē yǒu jiào wú lèi

Confucius said: "I teach everyone without discrimination."
(On Duke Ling of Wei 15.39)

Inspiration

Confucius is not a teacher who practised favouritism among his students. He adapted his teaching methods to different students. Zi Lu was an impatient student. Confucius told him to consult his parents first before taking any action. As for Ran Qiu who was timid, Confucius instructed him to put into immediate action whatever correct teachings he had learnt.

子曰：“君子不器。”　　《为政2.12》
zǐ yuē　jūn zǐ bù qì

Confucius said: "A gentleman is not like a utensil (having specific and limited uses)." (On Governing 2.12)

Inspiration

Zi Gong asked Confucius about his opinion about him. Confucius said: "You are like a utensil used for sacrificial purposes." By this, Confucius meant that Zi Gong was a talent indeed, but not an all-rounder.

子曰："后生可畏，焉知来者之不如今也？四十、
zǐ yuē hòu shēng kě wèi yān zhī lái zhě zhī bù rú jīn yě sì shí

五十而无闻焉，斯亦不足畏也已！"《子罕9.23》
wǔ shí ér wú wén yān sī yì bù zú wèi yě yǐ

Confucius said: "Young people are full of potential. Who can predict if they will not surpass our generation? But if by the age of 40 or 50, a person does not establish a name for himself, he will never do so."

(The Master Seldom 9.23)

Inspiration

There is an oft-quoted saying, "An idle youth, a needy age." To Confucius, as long as a youth is determined to work hard, he will surely have a bright future. However, if half of your life has already gone by with nothing achieved, you are not likely to go far. Confucius is, therefore, justified in saying: "If, at the age of 40, a man remains loathsome, he is done for."

TRUE ESSENCE OF FILIAL PIETY AND BENEVOLENCE

The character of 孝 (*xiao*, filial piety) consists of an upper 老 (*lao*, old) and a lower 子 (*zi*, child). Graphically, it indicates a child having an old man on his back, which means to take care of the elderly. Filial piety is more than material provision but also sincere respect and obedience.A person of filial piety will naturally have a heart for benevolence. A person of benevolence and virtues is like a piece of magnet. He does not need to declare his virtues. Inspired by his virtuous qualities, people will be drawn to him.

子曰：“里仁为美。择不处仁，焉得知*？”
zǐ yuē lǐ rén wéi měi zé bù chǔ rén yān dé zhì

《里仁4.1》

Confucius said: "The excellence of a neighbourhood is in its virtuous, moral life. If a man does not choose to reside in a neighbourhood where such moral living prevails, how can he be counted as one who is wise?"

(On Virtue 4.1)

Inspiration

To ensure that Mencius grew up in an healthy environment, his mother moved her home several times from near a graveyard, a noisy marketplace to finally a school. When Mencius saw students reading books, he also followed suit. Perhaps Mencius's mother was also influenced by this saying of Confucius.

*知：智

子曰：“不仁者，不可以久处约，不可以长处乐。
zǐ yuē bù rén zhě bù kě yǐ jiǔ chǔ yuē bù kě yǐ cháng chǔ lè

仁者安仁，知*者利仁。” 《里仁4.2》
rén zhě ān rén zhì zhě lì rén

Confucius said: "A man without virtue cannot endure adversity nor enjoy prosperity for long. A man of virtue rests content in virtue; a man of wisdom knows the way to gain the benefits of virtue." (On Virtue 4.2)

Inspiration

Confucius said: "A virtuous man has no worries." If a man lives by the principle of benevolence, he will have a happy life no matter the circumstances. In contrast, a man with no moral character remains insatiable at all times. He will grumble when poor and crave for more when rich.

*知：智

子曰："德不孤，必有邻。" 《里仁4.25》
zǐ yuē dé bù gū bì yǒu lín

Confucius said: "A virtuous man is never lonely. Others who are like-minded are bound to be drawn to him." (On Virtue 4.25)

Inspiration

Suppose there are two persons here. One is considerate in everything while the other is self-centred. Whom will you choose as your friend? Most of us will choose the first person. A benevolent person is like a piece of magnet. People are drawn to him because of his benevolent words and actions.

子曰："夫仁者，己欲立而立人，己欲达
zǐ yuē fú rén zhě jǐ yù lì ér lì rén jǐ yù dá

而达人。" 《雍也6.30》
ér dá rén

Confucius said: "A benevolent person is one who helps others to be established even as he establishes himself; who helps others to achieve even as he strives towards personal achievements." (About Yong Ye 6.30)

Inspiration

It is natural for man to be selfish. We do not help others unless we think we have extra time or energy. In fact, to help others accomplish success is also to help ourselves because other people are more likely to help us when we are considerate.

子曰：“仁远乎哉？我欲仁，斯仁至矣！”
zǐ yuē rén yuǎn hū zāi wǒ yù rén sī rén zhì yǐ

《述而7.30》

Confucius said: " Is benevolence very far from us? If we truly desire it, we can reach it." (On Transmitting 7.30)

Inspiration

Human beings are benevolent by nature. We all hanker for truth, benevolence and beauty. Actually, benevolence does not lie in the distance. Rather, it resides in our heart, waiting to do our bidding.

厩焚。子退朝，曰："伤人乎？"不问马。
jiù fén zǐ tuì cháo yuē shāng rén hū bú wèn mǎ

《乡党10. 17》

When his stables caught fire, Confucius took leave from court. The first thing he asked was "Has anyone been hurt?" instead of asking about his horses. (When in the Village 10.17)

Inspiration

Suppose your house is on fire one day. There are a piece of treasured painting and a cat inside. Which one would you save first?

子曰：“克己复礼为仁……非礼勿视，非礼勿听，
zǐ yuē kè jǐ fù lǐ wéi rén fēi lǐ wù shì fēi lǐ wù tīng

非礼勿言，非礼勿动。” 《颜渊12.1》
fēi lǐ wù yán fēi lǐ wù dòng

Confucius said: "To be able to overcome your desire and observe the rites in living; this is benevolence. Do not look at anything that does not accord with the rites. Do not listen to anything that does not accord with the rites. Do not say anything that does not accord with the rites. Do not do anything that does not accord with the rites." (On Yan Yuan 12.1)

Inspiration

"Do not look at what contradicts the proprieties; do not listen to what violates the proprieties; do not say what goes against the proprieties; and do not engage in what is contrary to the proprieties." Yet, at times, we still violate the proprieties. Thus, to overcome one's desires is as difficult as to rein in a wild horse.

樊迟问仁。子曰："爱人。"问知*。子曰：
fán chí wèn rén zǐ yuē ài rén wèn zhì zǐ yuē

"知人。"樊迟未达。子曰："举直错诸枉，
zhī rén fán chí wèi dá zǐ yuē jǔ zhí cuò zhū wǎng

能使枉者直。" 《颜渊12.22》
néng shǐ wǎng zhě zhí

Fan Chi asked:"What is benevolence?" Confucius said: "Love people." Fan Chi asked further: "What is wisdom?" Confucius said: "Know people." Seeing that Fan Chi still could not understand, Confucius said: "Elevate the righteous and expose the wicked, and the wicked will be made righteous."

(On Yan Yuan 12.22)

Inspiration

Emperor Tang of the Shang dynasty ruled the country by benevolence. His cook Yin Yi told him that state administration was just like cooking and all flavourings had to be mixed appropriately. Believing Yin Yi was a capable man, he appointed him as Prime Minister regardless of his humble origin. With his help, Emperor Tang successfully unified the country.

*知：智

子曰：“有德者必有言，有言者不必有德。
zǐ yuē yǒu dé zhě bì yǒu yán yǒu yán zhě bú bì yǒu dé

仁者必有勇，勇者不必有仁。” 《宪问14.4》
rén zhě bì yǒu yǒng yǒng zhě bú bì yǒu rén

Confucius said: “A virtuous man has great sayings, but those with great sayings are not always virtuous. A benevolent man is courageous, but those with great courage may not always be benevolent.” (Xian Questions 14.4)

Inspiration

A benevolent man possesses the courage of “sacrificing himself for the sake of benevolence”. However, courage if not coupled with benevolence may be inappropriately applied.

或曰：“以德报怨，何如？”子曰：“何以报德？
huò yuē yǐ dé bào yuàn hé rú zǐ yuē hé yǐ bào dé

以直报怨，以德报德。” 《宪问14.34》
yǐ zhí bào yuàn yǐ dé bào dé

Someone asked Confucius: “What do you think if one repays hatred with kindness?” Confucius said: “What then do you return kindness with? Repay hatred with justice, and repay kindness with kindness.” (Xian Questions 14.34)

Inspiration

“Returning like for like” or returning resentment with resentment will only lead to a vicious cycle. Yet, at the same time, we should not go so far in rectifying this because appeasement will only further fuel resentment.

子贡问曰：“有一言而可以终身行之者乎？”
zǐ gòng wèn yuē yǒu yī yán ér kě yǐ zhōng shēn xíng zhī zhě hū

子曰：“其恕乎！己所不欲，勿施于人。”
zǐ yuē qí shù hū jǐ suǒ bú yù wù shī yú rén

《卫灵公15.24》

Zi Gong asked: "Is there a single word that one can follow as a life principle?" Confucius: "Yes! It is perhaps 'consideration'. Do not do unto others what you do not want others to do unto you." (On Duke Ling of Wei 15.24)

Inspiration

The structure of Chinese characters is very interesting. Let us look at the character of "恕" (*shu*, forgiving). The upper part is "如" (*ru*, like) and the lower part "心" (*xin*, heart). Together, they are "如心" (meaning "like heart or sympathy"). You should treat others with sincerity from your heart and ask yourself: "Do I also hope that other people will treat me in the same way?"

子曰："巧言令色，鲜矣仁。" 《阳货17.17》
zǐ yuē qiǎo yán lìng sè xiǎn yǐ rén

Confucius said: "Those with flattering lips and who pretend to be kind do not possess benevolence." (On Yang Huo 17.17)

Inspiration

Those who know nothing but flatteries do not have self-esteem. A person without self-esteem has no sense of shame. He is immoral and cannot win the trust of others.

有子曰："其为人也孝弟*，而好犯上者，鲜矣；
yǒu zǐ yuē qí wéi rén yě xiào tì ér hào fàn shàng zhě xiǎn yǐ

不好犯上，而好作乱者，未之有也。君子务本，
bú hào fàn shàng ér hào zuò luàn zhě wèi zhī yǒu yě jūn zǐ wù běn

本立而道生。孝弟*也者，其为仁之本与！"
běn lì ér dào shēng xiào tì yě zhě qí wéi rén zhī běn yú

《学而1.2》

You Zi said: "A man who is filial to his parents and respects his elder brothers is seldom disposed to rebel against the authorities. He who is not disposed to rebel against the authorities will not be disposed to stir up chaos and create confusion. The gentleman devotes his attention to building the foundation of life. When this is firmly established, the Way is naturally conceived. Filial piety and fraternal respect—these are indeed the foundation and the roots of virtue and benevolence!" (On Learning 1.2)

Inspiration

We are grateful to our parents because it is they who bore and nurtured us. Filial piety is a basic moral principle. Even adult birds and beasts know how to feed their old mothers, let alone human beings.

子曰："父在观其志，父没观其行。三年无
zǐ yuē fù zài guān qí zhì fù mò guān qí xíng sān nián wú

改于父之道，可谓孝矣。" 《学而1.11》
gǎi yú fù zhī dào kě wèi xiào yǐ

Confucius said: "When a man's father is alive, check his aspirations. When a man's father is deceased, observe his conduct. If he did not waver from the promises made and principles taught by his father after three years of his father's death, he can be said to be a filial son." (On Learning 1.11)

Inspiration

Filial piety is not something to show off. It is not superficial respect and obedience. Rather, it is born out of a sincere heart.

子游问孝。子曰："今之孝者，是谓能养。
zǐ yóu wèn xiào zǐ yuē jīn zhī xiào zhě shì wèi néng yǎng

至于犬马，皆能有养。不敬，何以别乎？"
zhì yú quǎn mǎ jiē néng yǒu yǎng bú jìng hé yǐ bié hū

《为政2.7》

Zi You consulted Confucius about filial piety. Confucius said: "These days, meeting the physical needs of parents is considered filial piety. But even dogs and horses are likewise cared for. What difference is there if one does not show his parents respect?" (On Governing 2.7)

Inspiration

The Chinese character "孝" (*xiao*, filial piety) consists of an upper "老" (*lao*, old) and a lower "子" (*zi*, child). Graphically, it indicates a child having an old man on his back, which means to take care of the elderly. Caring for one's parents means not only material provision but also sincere respect and obedience towards them.

子曰："事父母几谏，见志不从，又敬不违，
zǐ yuē shì fù mǔ jī jiàn jiàn zhì bù cóng yòu jìng bù wéi

劳而不怨。" 《里仁4.18》
láo ér bú yuàn

Confucius said: "When pointing out the errors of one's parents, be gentle. When they refuse to heed your advice, remain respectful. Be concerned, but do not harbour bitterness." (On Virtue 4.18)

Inspiration

Once Zeng Can's father beat him with a wooden club severely. Confucius told him: "You should allow your father to beat you if he uses a small club, but run away when he uses a big club. Otherwise, if you die, your father will end up being an unbenevolent man." This story tells us that what Confucius advocated is not "stupid filial piety".

子曰：“父母在，不远游。游必有方。”
zǐ yuē fù mǔ zài bù yuǎn yóu yóu bì yǒu fāng

《里仁4.19》

Confucius said: "When your parents are alive, avoid going on long journeys. If you must do so, you should always let them know where you are going."
(On Virtue 4.19)

Inspiration

Xu Xiake (1586-1641) was a prominent traveller and geographer of the Ming Dynasty. Since young, it was his ambition to travel across the country. His mother told him not to worry about her and encouraged him to go and realise his dream. Gradually, he started to go on long-distance journeys. This is a good example of filial piety.

子曰：“父母之年，不可不知也。一则以喜，
zǐ yuē fù mǔ zhī nián bù kě bù zhī yě yì zé yǐ xǐ

一则以惧。”
yì zé yǐ jù

《里仁4.21》

Confucius said: “One should always remember the birthdays of one’s parents. On the one hand, their longevity is a cause for celebration but on the other hand, their old age is a cause for concern.” (On Virtue 4.21)

Inspiration

“The trees want to remain quiet, but the wind will not subside. I want to take care of my parents, but they have already passed away.” We should fulfil our filial duties as early as possible while our parents are still around. It is much better to spend more time with them than to have a grand funeral after they pass away.

子 夏 曰 ： “ 君 子 敬 而 无 失 ， 与 人 恭 而 有 礼 ，
zǐ xià yuē jūn zǐ jìng ér wú shī yǔ rén gōng ér yǒu lǐ

四 海 之 内 皆 兄 弟 也 。 君 子 何 患 乎 无 兄 弟 也 ？ ”
sì hǎi zhī nèi jiē xiōng dì yě jūn zǐ hé huàn hū wú xiōng dì yě

《颜渊12.5》

Zi Xia said: “If a gentleman is excellent in his work, does nothing wrong and treat people respectfully, he will make all men his brothers. So, why should a gentleman worry that he has no brothers?” (On Yan Yuan 12.5)

Inspiration

“All men are brothers.” A true brother is not merely a title or a form of address. It also implies mutual aid between people. As long as you treat others sincerely and honestly, you can even find your brothers among people who are not your kith and kin.

THE IDEAL PERSONALITY

A gentleman embodies the ideal personality. Directly opposed to the gentleman is the petty man. A gentleman can sacrifice his life for the moral principles he believes in and "does what he knows is impossible to achieve". He clings firmly to his faith without regret. Therefore, the gentleman is able to live with poverty, adhere to the Way and remain magnanimous in all situations.

子曰：“君子怀德，小人怀土。君子怀刑，
zǐ yuē jūn zǐ huái dé xiǎo rén huái tǔ jūn zǐ huái xíng

小人怀惠。” 《里仁4.11》
xiǎo rén huái huì

Confucius said: “The gentleman cherishes virtue, but the petty man cherishes his own home. A gentleman is concerned about law and justice, but the petty man is only preoccupied with self-interest.” (On Virtue 4.11)

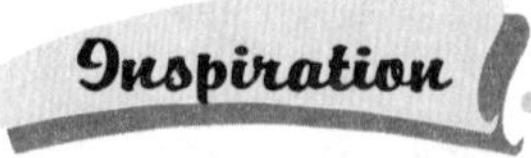

A gentleman does not merely care about himself. He also concerns himself with the society.

子曰："君子喻于义，小人喻于利。"
zǐ yuē jūn zǐ yù yú yì xiǎo rén yù yú lì

《里仁4.16》

Confucius said: "The gentleman considers righteousness; the petty man considers only gain." (On Virtue 4.16)

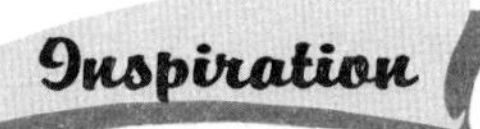

The ancient Greek sage Solon said that morality is permanent while wealth changes its owner everyday. Therefore, a man who knows what life truly means will pursue permanent values instead of transitory gains.

子谓子夏曰：“女* 为君子儒，无为小人儒。”
zǐ wèi zǐ xià yuē rǔ wéi jūn zǐ rú wú wéi xiǎo rén rú

《雍也6.13》

Confucius said to Zi Xia: "You should be a scholar with impeccable morals, not a scholar who lacks integrity." (About Yong Ye 6.13)

Inspiration

A gentleman is able to practise what is difficult while a petty man acts wilfully. A gentleman chooses an arduous way, while a petty man takes a well-trodden one. Which way will you choose for yourself?

*女：同“汝”。

子曰："君子坦荡荡，小人长戚戚。"
zǐ yuē jūn zi tǎn dàng dàng xiǎo rén cháng qì qì

《述而7.37》

Confucius said: "A gentleman is magnanimous and free; a petty man is mean-spirited and fretful." (On Transmitting 7.37)

Inspiration

A spiritually rich man does not worry about loss and gain. Someone asked the great Western philosopher Socrates why he could remain in high spirits all the time. Socrates answered: "I do not have anything whose loss may make me sad."

子 曰 ： “ 君 子 成 人 之 美 ， 不 成 人 之 恶 。
zǐ yuē jūn zǐ chéng rén zhī měi bù chéng rén zhī è

小 人 反 是 ！ 《颜渊12.16》
xiǎo rén fǎn shì

Confucius said: “A gentleman helps others to succeed and never causes them to fail. A petty man does the opposite.” (On Yan Yuan 12.16)

Inspiration

Sometimes, helping other people to succeed is actually helping yourself to succeed. Turning a blind eye to the achievements of others only reveals your narrow-mindedness.

子曰：“君子上达，小人下达。” 《子路14.23》

zǐ yuē jūn zǐ shàng dá xiǎo rén xià dá

Confucius said: “A gentleman has lofty ambitions; a petty man has basely aims.” (Xian Questions 14.23)

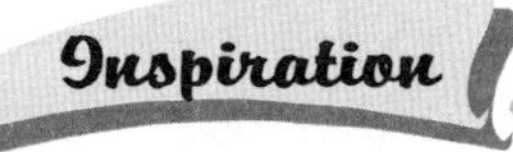

What you seeks determines the worth of your life.

子曰："君子义以为质，礼以行之，孙* 以出之，
zǐ yuē jūn zǐ yì yǐ wéi zhì lǐ yǐ xíng zhī xùn yǐ chū zhī

信以成之。君子哉！" 《卫灵公15.18》
xìn yǐ chéng zhī jūn zǐ zāi

Confucius said: "When one abides by righteousness as a principle of life, adheres to the rites, speaks with modesty and is trustworthy in all his ways, he may be regarded as a true gentleman." (On Duke Ling of Wei 15.18)

Inspiration

A modest gentleman is not someone sporting merely a modest look. His modesty and politeness is an embedded part of his personality.

*孙：同"逊"。

孔子曰：“君子有九思：视思明，听思聪，色思温，
kǒng zǐ yuē jūn zǐ yǒu jiǔ sī shì sī míng tīng sī cōng sè sī wēn

貌思恭，言思忠，事思敬，疑思问，忿思难，
mào sī gōng yán sī zhōng shì sī jìng yí sī wèn fèn sī nàn

见得思义。”
jiàn dé sī yì

《季氏16.10》

Confucius said: “There are nine things which a gentleman is mindful of: when looking, has he seen clearly; when listening, has he understood correctly; in facial expressions, does he reflect gentleness; in mannerism, is he courteous; when speaking, is he sincere; at work, is he conscientious; when in doubt, does he seek advice; when angry, has he considered the consequences; when he sees a gain, does he ponder whether he deserves it.”

(The Chief of the Ji Family 16.10)

Inspiration

What consequences will your words and actions have? Keeping this in mind regularly will prevent you from doing things you regret.

子贡曰：“君子之过也，如日月之食焉：过也，
zǐ gòng yuē jūn zǐ zhī guò yě rú rì yuè zhī shí yān guò yě

人皆见之；更也，人皆仰之。” 《子张19.21》
rén jiē jiàn zhī gēng yě rén jiē yǎng zhī

Zi Gong said: "A gentleman's errors are like an eclipse of the sun and the moon: When he errs, the whole world can see it. When he amends his ways, the whole world looks up to him." (On Zi Zhang 19.21)

Inspiration

A gentleman is a role model for the public and also the cynosure of public attention. His actions and words are "magnified".

子曰："道不行，乘桴浮于海。从我者其由
zǐ yuē dào bù xíng chéng fú fú yú hǎi cóng wǒ zhě qí yóu

与？"子路闻之喜。子曰："由也，好勇过
yú zǐ lù wén zhī xǐ zǐ yuē yóu yě hào yǒng guò

我，无所取材。" 《公冶长5.7》
wǒ wú suǒ qǔ cái

Confucius said: "If my way does not work, I will take a small boat and travel far out to sea. There is only one person who will faithfully follow me. That is Zhong You." Zi Lu became very happy when he heard this.
Confucius continued: "Perhaps Zhong You has more courage than me, but he does not seem to have any other abilities." (On Gong Ye Zhang 5.7)

Inspiration

Before formally acknowledging Confucius as his teacher, Zi Lu did not like him. Confucius treated him politely and won him over with eloquent arguments. Zi Lu became convinced and declared Confucius his mentor. Henceforth, Zi Lu became very loyal to his mentor and was always ready to defend Confucius.

曾子曰：“可以托六尺之孤，可以寄百里之命，
zēng zǐ yuē kě yǐ tuō liù chǐ zhī gū kě yǐ jì bǎi lǐ zhī mìng

临大节而不可夺也。君子人与？君子人也。”
lín dà jié ér bù kě duó yě jūn zǐ rén yú jūn zǐ rén yě

《泰伯8.6》

Zeng Zi said: “Someone who can be entrusted with the care of a young ruler, who can shoulder the responsibilities of guarding a strategic territory, and remains unyielding in a major crisis, is he a gentleman? Yes, indeed he is!”
(On Tai Bo 8.6)

Inspiration

Zhuge Liang of the Three Kingdoms Period helped Liu Bei build the Kingdom of Shu. Before Liu Bei died, he put his son in Zhuge Liang's custody. Although the young emperor was not worthy of support at all, Zhuge Liang till his death still made his utmost effort to assist him.

** One li is about half a kilometre.*

曾子曰："士不可以不弘毅，任重而道远，
zēng zǐ yuē shì bù kě yǐ bù hóng yì rèn zhòng ér dào yuǎn

仁以为己任，不亦重乎？死而后已，不亦远乎？"
rén yǐ wéi jǐ rèn bú yì zhòng hū sǐ ěr hòu yǐ bú yì yuǎn hū

《泰伯8.7》

Zeng Zi said: "A learned man must be strong and steadfast, for his responsibilities are heavy and the road is long. He must make it his responsibility to be benevolent—isn't that a heavy burden to bear? And he must maintain this till he dies—isn't that a long way to go?" (On Tai Bo 8.7)

Inspiration

The great French writer Victor Hugo said: "When our hearts have a huge dragon, it is both a tough punishment and joy." This huge dragon refers to a grand goal. With such a goal in mind, one will feel happy even in adverse circumstances.

子曰：“譬如为山，未成一篑，止，吾止也。
zǐ yuē pì rú wéi shān wèi chéng yī kuì zhǐ wú zhǐ yě

譬如平地，虽覆一篑，进，吾往也。”
pì rú píng dì suī fù yī kuì jìn wú wǎng yě

《子罕9.19》

Confucius said: "Just like building a mound, if there is one last basket of earth to be poured in but I choose to stop, the job is not completed. Just like levelling the ground, if only the first basket of earth has been poured in but I choose to persevere, the job will eventually be completed."

(The Master Seldom 9.19)

Inspiration

Life is a process of seeking progress nonstop. Like flowing water, progress brings vitality. An inactive life, in contrast, is no different from a pond of stagnant water.

子曰：“三军可夺帅也，匹夫不可夺志也。”
zǐ yuē sān jūn kě duó shuài yě pǐ fū bù kě duó zhì yě

《子罕9.26》

Confucius said: “The army may lose its commander, but a man cannot lose his aspirations.” (The Master Seldom 9.26)

Inspiration

Su Dongpo is a great poet of the Song dynasty. He once said: “Those who accomplish great things since olden times do not only have extraordinary talents but also a firm and indomitable will.” In other words, a person without great ambition will find it very hard to succeed in anything.

子曰：“岁寒，然后知松柏之后雕*也。”
zǐ yuē suì hán rán hòu zhī sōng bǎi zhī hòu diāo yě

《子罕9.28》

Confucius said: “Only in winter can one see that the cypress and the pine are the last to shed their leaves.” (The Master Seldom 9.28)

Inspiration

One's moral integrity can only go through a true test in adverse circumstances. “Unless the cold wind pierces their bones, plum blossoms won't become so fragrant.” Only after a rigorous moulding process can one's character be developed.

*雕：同“凋”。

子曰：“知* 者不惑，仁者不忧，勇者不惧。”
zǐ yuē zhì zhě bù huò rén zhě bù yōu yǒng zhě bù jù

《子罕9.29》

Confucius said: “The wise is never confused. The benevolent is never worried. The courageous is never afraid.” (The Master Seldom 9.29)

Inspiration

Equipped with wisdom, benevolence and courage, a person will succeed in everything he does throughout his life.

*知：智

子路宿于石门。晨门曰："奚自？"子路曰："自孔氏。"
zǐ lù sù yú shí mén chén mén yuē xī zì zǐ lù yuē zì kǒng shì

曰："是知其不可而为之者与？"《宪问14.38》
yuē shì zhī qí bù kě ér wéi zhī zhě yú

Zi Lu lodged at the Stone Gate. The next morning, the gatekeeper questioned him: "Where did you come from?" Zi Lu replied: "I am Confucius's disciple." The gatekeeper said: "Is he the one who knows it cannot be done yet keeps trying?" (Xian Questions 14.38)

Inspiration

A man may apply himself persistently to something clearly impossible. This results from his solid conviction that what he seeks after is right, beautiful and completely worthwhile.

子曰："志士仁人，无求生以害仁，有
zǐ yuē zhì shì rén rén wú qiú shēng yǐ hài rén yǒu

杀身以成仁。" 《卫灵公15.9》
shā shēn yǐ chéng rén

Confucius said: "A righteous man would not compromise benevolence because he fears death, but would give up his life to uphold benevolence."
(On Duke Ling of Wei 15.9)

Inspiration

German writer Friedrich von Schille said: "A brave man risks his life, but not his conscience." To a man with moral courage, life is very valuable indeed. Yet, he would give his life up when necessary. What he cannot give up is his values.

子曰：“当仁，不让于师。” 《卫灵公15.36》
zǐ yuē dāng rén bú ràng yú shī

Confucius said: “When the occasion calls for practising benevolence, you don’t have to give way, even to your teacher.” (On Duke Ling of Wei 15.36)

Inspiration

In terms of the virtue of benevolence, we should not relent at all to criticize a teacher who has made a mistake. Benevolence is the ultimate criterion for judging good and evil.

子曰：“道不同，不相为谋。”《卫灵公15.40》
zǐ yuē dào bù tóng bù xiāng wéi móu

Confucius said: "People of different values cannot work on a venture together."
(On Duke Ling of Wei 15.40)

Inspiration

You can still make friends with people who have different hobbies and goals. However, it is very hard for people with different ideals to accomplish something jointly.

子张曰：“士见危致命，见得思义，祭思敬，
zǐ zhāng yuē shì jiàn wēi zhì mìng jiàn dé sī yì jì sī jìng

丧思哀，其可已矣。” 《子张19.1》
sāng sī āi qí kě yǐ yǐ

Zi Zhang said: “A learned man, in the face of danger, is willing to lay down his life; when presented with an opportunity for gain, thinks whether it is right; in offering sacrifices, does it with great reverence; in mourning, expresses heartfelt grief. If he could do these, he would have done all that is necessary.”
(On Zi Zhang 19.1)

Inspiration

A person must be careful with his words and actions. He cannot make progress unless he is strict with himself.

SELF-EXAMINATION AND PRECAUTION

Self-examination leads to self-improvement. Every night, a person should examine himself on what he has said, what he has done and what he has thought about. The purpose is to see if he has done anything wrong, if he has said anything unreasonable and if he has had any wrong thoughts. Where there has been any wrong action, words or thoughts, he can then rectify it. Thus, he will make daily progress. Self-examination can also serve as a precaution against anything that may lead us astray.

曾子曰："吾日三省吾身：为人谋而不忠乎？
zēng zǐ yuē wú rì sān xǐng wú shēn wèi rén móu ér bù zhōng hū

与朋友交而不信乎？传不习乎？" 《学而1.4》
yǔ péng yǒu jiāo ér bú xìn hū chuán bù xí hū

Zeng Zi said: "Daily, I examine myself in three areas. Have I done my best when doing things for others? Have I been been trustworthy in my dealings with my friends? Have I revised the lessons I have been taught?"

(On Learning 1.4)

Inspiration

It is good to be self-conscious. A self-conscious man examines himself from time to time. He corrects his mistakes and encourages himself to work harder for further growth.

子曰：“见贤思齐焉，见不贤而内自省也。”
zǐ yuē jiàn xián sī qí yān jiàn bù xián ér nèi zì xǐng yě

《里仁4.17》

Confucius said: "When one meets a man of virtue and great talent, one should look to him as an example to learn from. When one meets a man without virtue or talent, one should reflect on whether one also has similar flaws." (On Virtue 4.17)

Inspiration

Don't be jealous of others who possess admirable qualities. We should learn from them and work hard to catch up with them. Don't scorn others for their shortcomings. Rather, we should guard ourselves against those undesirable aspects.

子曰：“已矣乎！吾未见能见其过而内自讼者
zǐ yuē yǐ yǐ hū wú wèi jiàn néng jiàn qí guò ér nèi zì sòng zhě

也。” 《公冶长5.27》
yě

Confucius said: “Forget it! I’ve not seen anyone who could criticize his own faults.” (On Gong Ye Zhang 5.27)

Inspiration

We tend to blame others for their mistakes. Yet, when we make any errors, we would defend ourselves with all possible excuses. Self-criticism and examination demand us to have the courage to face up to ourselves.

子绝四：毋意，毋必，毋固，毋我。
zǐ jué sì wú yì wú bì wú gù wú wǒ

《子罕9.4》

Confucius' four abstinences are not making wild conjectures, not being dogmatic, not being obstinate and not being arrogant.

(The Master Seldom 9.4)

Inspiration

If you add water to a full cup, the water will overflow. You cannot refill the cup until you empty it. Let us be an "empty" cup in order to take in new things.

子夏为莒父宰，问政。子曰：“无欲速，
zǐ xià wéi jǔ fù zǎi wèn zhèng zǐ yuē wú yù sù

无见小利。欲速则不达，见小利则大事不成。”
wú jiàn xiǎo lì yù sù zé bù dá jiàn xiǎo lì zé dà shì bù chéng

《**子路**13. 17》

When Zi Xia became country magistrate of Jufu county, he asked Confucius about government.
Confucius said: “Do not be hasty and do not covet small gains. Being too much in a hurry may result in one not reaching the goal, and coveting small gains will result in one not achieving anything big.” (On Zi Lu 13.17)

Inspiration

Ancient Greek poet Euripides told his friend, “I have finished three lines of poetry in three days.” His friend said, “I can write at least one hundred lines in three days.” Euripedes replied, “Yes, you can do that. But what you write has a lifespan of three days at most.”

子曰：“巧言乱德。小不忍，则乱大谋。”
zǐ yuē qiǎo yán luàn dé xiǎo bù rěn zé luàn dà móu

《卫灵公15.27》

Confucius said: “A glib tongue ruins one’s moral virtues. Intolerance for small mistakes puts plans in jeopardy.” (On Duke Ling of Wei 15.27)

Inspiration

Those who accomplish grand exploits since olden times possess the virtues of fortitude and tolerance. Marshal Han Xin helped Liu Bang or Emperor Gaozu of Han conquer the country and founded the Han dynasty. When he was young he once put up with a rascal’s provocation, thus preserving his life for larger and more meaningful things.

子曰：“过而不改，是谓过矣。”
zǐ yuē guò ér bù gǎi shì wèi guò yǐ

《卫灵公15.30》

Confucius said: “To make a mistake and not correct it is a mistake indeed.”
(On Duke Ling of Wei 15.30)

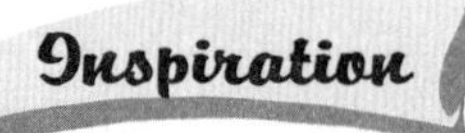

Inspiration

To err is human. Even sages make mistakes. Nobody is infallible in this world. What is important is that you correct yourself when you realise you are wrong, and take timely measures to improve yourself.

孔子曰："益者三乐，损者三乐。乐节礼乐，
kǒng zǐ yuē yì zhě sān lè sǔn zhě sān lè lè jié lǐ yuè

乐道人之善，乐多贤友，益矣。乐骄乐，
lè dào rén zhī shàn lè duō xián yǒu yì yǐ lè jiāo lè

乐佚游，乐宴乐，损矣。" 《季氏16.5》
lè yì yóu lè yàn lè sǔn yǐ

Confucius said: "There are three kinds of healthy preoccupations and also three kinds of unhealthy preoccupations. The healthy preoccupations include cultivation through the rites and music, praising the virtues of another and enjoying the company of the virtuous. The unhealthy preoccupations include being arrogant about one's position, loafing, and being gluttonous."

(The Chief of the Ji Family 16.5)

Inspiration

We all pursue joy and happiness. The question is: Are all forms of joy and happiness good or worthy of our effort? This is no different from our attitude towards pain. All of us are afraid of pain, but there are some kinds of pain we need not run away from.

孔子曰：“侍于君子有三愆：言未及之而言
kǒng zǐ yuē shì yú jūn zǐ yǒu sān qiān yán wèi jí zhī ér yán

谓之躁，言及之而不言谓之隐，未见颜色而
wèi zhī zào yán jí zhī ér bù yán wèi zhī yǐn wèi jiàn yán sè ér

言谓之瞽。”《季氏16.6》
yán wèi zhī gǔ

Confucius said: “When attending to gentlemen, three errors are possible: speaking when it is not time, which is being hasty; keeping quiet when it is time to speak, which is being secretive; and speaking first without watching a listener's expression, which is being blind.”

(The Chief of the Ji Family 16.6)

Inspiration

Speaking is the most direct mode of communication between people. Yet, there are many who speak to themselves.

孔子曰："君子有三戒：少之时，血气未定，
kǒng zǐ yuē jūn zǐ yǒu sān jiè shào zhī shí xuè qì wèi dìng

戒之在色；及其壮也，血气方刚，戒之在斗；
jiè zhī zài sè jí qí zhuàng yě xuè qì fāng gāng jiè zhī zài dòu

及其老也，血气既衰，戒之在得。" 《季氏16.7》
jí qí lǎo yě xuè qì jì shuāi jiè zhī zài dé

Confucius said: "A gentleman should guard against three things. In one's youth, when the vital energy (*qi*) is underdeveloped, refrain from lusting after the opposite sex. When one has matured, and the vital energy is at the prime, refrain from being bellicose. When one is old and the vital energy is waning, refrain from avarice." (The Chief of the Ji Family 16.7)

Inspiration

There are crucial junctures at each stage of our life. Only when we rise to the challenge at these injunctures can we enjoy a meaningful life.

孔子曰："君子有三畏：畏天命，畏大人，
kǒng zǐ yuē jūn zǐ yǒu sān wèi wèi tiān mìng wèi dà rén

畏圣人之言。小人不知天命而不畏也，
wèi shèng rén zhī yán xiǎo rén bù zhī tiān mìng ér bú wèi yě

狎大人，侮圣人之言。" 《季氏16.8》
xiá dà rén wǔ shèng rén zhī yán

Confucius said: "A gentleman stands in awe of three things. He stands in awe of the will of heaven, great men and the words of wise men. A petty man does not respect heaven's will, great men or the words of wise men."
(The Chief of the Ji Family 16.8)

Inspiration

It is not true courage for someone to have no idea of "the immensity of the universe" and who is not in awe of anything. Without an awe-struck heart, a man may not hesitate at all to commit evil acts.

子曰：“躬自厚而薄责于人，则远怨矣。”
zǐ yuē gōng zì hòu ér bó zé yú rén zé yuǎn yuàn yǐ

《卫灵公15.15》

Confucius said: “Being strict with oneself and lenient with others saves one from ill will.” (On Duke Ling of Wei 15.15)

A person who is overly self-defensive is like a prickly hedgehog that stings people often.

子曰：“君子求诸己，小人求诸人。”
zǐ yuē jūn zǐ qiú zhū jǐ xiǎo rén qiú zhū rén

《卫灵公15.21》

Confucius said: “A gentleman is demanding with himself but a petty man is demanding towards others.” (On Duke Ling of Wei 15.21)

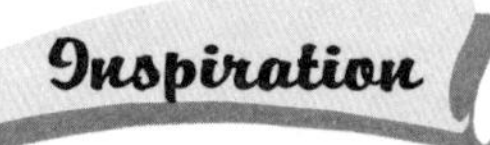

Inspiration

We are usually extremely strict with others and even a mistake the size of a grain of sand cannot escape our eyes. When it comes to ourselves, a mistake as visible as a wooden beam may go unnoticed.

子曰：“君子不以言举人，不以人废言。”
zǐ yuē jūn zǐ bù yǐ yán jǔ rén bù yǐ rén fèi yán

《卫灵公15.23》

Confucius said: “A gentleman will not be wheedled, nor will he reject the correct sayings of others even if they display some flaws in their character.”
(On Duke Ling of Wei 15.23)

Inspiration

To discern truth from falsehood, we should look beyond the surface appearance.

子曰："恭而无礼则劳，慎而无礼则葸，
zǐ yuē gōng ér wú lǐ zé láo shèn ér wú lǐ zé xǐ

勇而无礼则乱，直而无礼则绞。" 《泰伯8.2》
yǒng ér wú lǐ zé luàn zhí ér wú lǐ zé jiǎo

Confucius said: "Courtesy without following the rites leads to weariness. Being overly cautious without knowing the rites causes one to be timid. Courage without knowing the rites gets one into trouble. Frankness without knowing the rites causes hurt to others." (On Tai Bo 8.2)

Inspiration

Propriety does not refer to restraints or restrictions. Rather, it indicates a respect for oneself and others.

子贡问："师与商也孰贤？"子曰："师
zǐ gòng wèn shī yǔ shāng yě shú xián zǐ yuē shī

也过，商也不及。"曰："然则师愈与？"
yě guò shāng yě bù jí yuē rán zé shī yù yú

子曰："过犹不及。" 《先进11.16》
zǐ yuē guò yóu bù jí

Zi Gong asked: "Between Zhuansun Shi and Bu Shang, who is more virtuous and capable?" Confucius replied: "Zhuansun Shi tends to go too far in performing his tasks while Bu Shang tends not to go far enough."
Zi Gong said: "In that case, Zhuansun Shi is better." Confucius said: "Actually, going too far and not going far enough are just as bad."
(On the Forerunners 11.16)
Note: Confucius advocates the principle of *The Mean*.

Inspiration

The way of life is like cooking; too little or too much salt will not produce good dishes.

子温而厉，威而不猛，恭而安。 《述而7.38》

zǐ wēn ér lì wēi ér bù měng gōng ér ān

Confucius was gentle yet firm, commanding but not harsh, grave but calm.
(On Transmitting 7.38)

Inspiration

Only strings that are not so taut or so loose can produce sweet music. This principle also applies to our dealings with others.

子曰：“群居终日，言不及义，好行小慧，
zǐ yuē qún jū zhōng rì yán bù jí yì hào xíng xiǎo huì

难矣哉！”《卫灵公15.17》
nán yǐ zāi

Confucius said: “Those who gather for small talk all day long without speaking of what is right or true, but only to display their petty cleverness will not accomplish anything.” (On Duke Ling of Wei 15.17)

Inspiration

People like to gather to chat and kill time. Precious time thus elapses. Time is gold. If time can be measured by gold, would we still spend it like this?

子曰：“放*于利而行，多怨。” 《里仁4.12》

zǐ yuē fǎng yú lì ér xíng duō yuàn

Confucius said: “He who acts only with a view to his own advantage surely makes many enemies and invites much hatred.” (On Virtue 4.12)

Inspiration

He who keeps his mind fixed on earning money with no sense of benevolence, justice, honour or shame will never gain the support of others. Rather, he will incur public anger.

*放：“仿”。

LEADERSHIP AND PRACTICE

Confucius said, "To govern means to be upright. If you govern the people using upright principles, who will dare not to be upright?" A ruler who occupies the high position must set a good example for his subordinates. He is expected to take care of the people with a humane heart and educate them with virtuous acts. Only a ruler who puts into practice what he says can win the people's trust. However, this is easier said than done. Even Confucius dared not declare that he could always match his words with his actions.

子曰："为政以德，譬如北辰，居其所而众
zǐ yuē wéi zhèng yǐ dé pì rú běi chén jū qí suǒ ér zhòng

星共* 之。" 《为政2.1》
xīng gǒng zhī

Confucius said: "One who rules a high standard of morality is like the North star which stays firm while the other stars take reference from it."
(On Governing 2.1)

Inspiration

People will come and pledge their allegiance, of their own accord, to a monarch who is benevolent. Primarily because of their benevolent administration, sagacious monarchs in Chinese history, such as Emperor Wen of the Zhou dynasty and Emperor Tang of the Shang dynasty, gained strong support from the public and unified the country.

*共：同"拱"。

子曰："道*之以政，齐之以刑，民免而无耻；
zǐ yuē dǎo zhī yǐ zhèng qí zhī yǐ xíng mín miǎn ér wú chǐ

道*之以德，齐之以礼，有耻且格。"《为政2.3》
dǎo zhī yǐ dé qí zhī yǐ lǐ yǒu chǐ qiě gé

Confucius said: "If people are governed by laws, and order is maintained through punishment, then people will not do wrong but they will not have a sense of shame. If people are inspired by a moral and virtuous government, and order is maintained by rites of propriety, people will do good because they do not want to live with a sense of shame." (On Governing 2.3)

Inspiration

Like "the stone placed over the weeds", the criminal law is enacted to bring evil acts under control. When the stone is removed, criminal activities may rise again like the weeds. Only by imparting moral consciousness and cultivating the idea of shame can a person who is led astray reform himself thoroughly.

*道：导

哀公问曰：“何为则民服？”孔子对曰：
āi gōng wèn yuē hé wéi zé mín fú kǒng zǐ duì yuē

“举直错诸枉，则民服；举枉错诸直，
jǔ zhí cuò zhū wǎng zé mín fú jǔ wǎng cuò zhū zhí

则民不服。” 《为政2.19》
zé mín bù fú

Duke Ai of Lu asked Confucius: “How does one win the submission of the people?”
Confucius said: “Promote the righteous and suppress the wicked, the people will submit. Promote the wicked and suppress the righteous, the people will not submit.” (On Governing 2.19)

Inspiration

A leader should be able to recognise and use talents. Otherwise, how can he win the trust of others?

子曰："不在其位，不谋其政。" 《泰伯8.14》
zǐ yuē bú zài qí wèi bù móu qí zhèng

Confucius said: "Do not interfere with someone else's duties when one is not in their official position." (On Tai Bo 8.14)

Inspiration

Everybody has a job as well as corresponding functions and duties to fulfil within certain limits. If he oversteps the limits, the harmonious order will be broken.

子曰："足食、足兵，民信之矣……民无信不立。"
zǐ yuē zú shí zú bīng mín xìn zhī yǐ mín wú xìn bù lì

《颜渊12.7》

Confucius said: "To govern well, one must have sufficient food, an adequate army and the people's trust. Of these three, the people's trust is the most important. Without the people's trust, the government cannot stand."

(On Yan Yuan 12.7)

Inspiration

The people constitute the foundation of a country. If the ruler has the popular trust, he will be able to retain his leadership; if he loses the popular support, he will surely be overthrown by the people. The fall of many dynastic regimes in Chinese history is due in large part to rulers who had lost the popular trust.

君君，臣臣，父父，子子。 《颜渊12.11》

jūn jūn chén chén fù fù zǐ zǐ

Let the ruler be a ruler, the minister a minster, the father a father, and the son a son. (On Yan Yuan 12.11)

Inspiration

Social order and stability cannot be maintained unless each person performs the duties appropriate to his role.

季康子问政于孔子。孔子对曰："政者，
jì kāng zǐ wèn zhèng yú kǒng zǐ kǒng zǐ duì yuē zhèng zhě

正也。子帅以正，孰敢不正！" 《颜渊 12.17》
zhèng yě zǐ shuài yǐ zhèng shú gǎn bù zhèng

When Ji Kang Zi asked Confucius how one should govern, Confucius answered: "To govern means to be upright. If you lead the people in an upright way, who will dare to be corrupt?" (On Yan Yuan 12.17)

Inspiration

"When the upper beam is not straight, the lower one will also go aslant." If those in senior positions set a good example, those in subordinate positions will follow suit.

子曰：“其身正，不令而行；其身不正，
zǐ yuē qí shēn zhèng bú lìng ér xíng qí shēn bú zhèng

虽令不从。” 《子路13.6》
suī lìng bù cóng

Confucius said: "If the ruler is upright, even if he does not issue orders, people will follow him. But if the ruler is corrupt, even if he repeatedly issues orders, people will not follow." (On Zi Lu 13.6)

Inspiration

Confucius laid special emphasis on the administrators' moral cultivation. He illustrated this with the following: the administrators' work style is like the wind while the civilians act like the grass. The grass will bend in whichever direction the wind blows. Therefore, you must rectify yourself first before you are qualified to rectify others.

名不正，则言不顺；言不顺，则事不成；
míng bú zhèng zé yán bú shùn yán bú shùn zé shì bù chéng

事不成，则礼乐不兴；礼乐不兴，则刑罚不
shì bù chéng zé lǐ yuè bù xīng lǐ yuè bù xīng zé xíng fá bú

中；刑罚不中，则民无所措手足。《子路13.3》
zhòng xíng fá bú zhòng zé mín wú suǒ cuò shǒu zú

Without establishing proper titles, one's instructions will not be respected. When instructions are not followed, work will not get done. If work does not get done, then music and the rites cannot be implemented. If music and the rites are not implemented, law and punishment cannot be established. Then the people will not know how to live rightly. (On Zi Lu 13.3)

Inspiration

A "correct name" actually means something or somebody worthy of the name. If you cry out wine, and sell vinegar, is it possible to win the trust of others?

子适卫，冉有仆。子曰：“庶矣哉！”
zǐ shì wèi rǎn yǒu pú zǐ yuē shù yǐ zāi

冉有曰：“既庶矣，又何加焉？”曰：“富之。”
rǎn yǒu yuē jì shù yǐ yòu hé jiā yān yuē fù zhī

曰：“既富矣，又何加焉？”曰：“教之。”
yuē jì fù yǐ yòu hé jiā yān yuē jiào zhī

《子路13.9》

When Confucius went to the State of Wei, Ran You was his carriage driver. Confucius said: "The State of Wei has such a large population!" Ran You asked: "What then should be done?"
Confucius said: "Help them to become rich."
Ran You asked again: "After they have become rich, what then?" Confucius said: "Educate them." (On Zi Lu 13.9)

Inspiration

Guan Zhong, a well-known statesman of the Spring and Autumn Period, believed that the essence of state administration lies in how to conform to the popular will. Only when the people's well-being is improved, will they know the importance of abiding by the rituals and rites and pledging their allegiance to the administrators.

子曰：“吾与回言终日，不违，如愚。退而
zǐ yuē wú yǔ huí yán zhōng rì bù wéi rú yú tuì ér

省其私，亦足以发。回也不愚！” 《为政2.9》
xǐng qí sī yì zú yǐ fā huí yě bù yú

Confucius said: “For the whole day that I spoke to Yan Hui, he did not voice any disagreement. This makes him appear stupid. But I discovered that when he is studying in private, he does produce profound thoughts. This proves that he is not stupid at all.” (On Governing 2.9)

Inspiration

A persuasive discourse on an idea does not necessarily mean a true understanding. It is better to put it into practice.

子贡问君子。子曰："先行其言，而后从之。"

zǐ gòng wèn jūn zǐ　zǐ yuē　xiān xíng qí yán　ér hòu cóng zhī

《为政2.13》

Zi Gong asked Confucius about the nature of a true gentleman. Confucius said: "He does not preach what he practises till he has practised what he preaches." (On Governing 2.13)

A gentleman always acts on his ideas.

Before revealing it to others.

Inspiration

Your credit rests on whether you can honor your words.

子曰：“多闻阙疑，慎言其余。则寡尤；
zǐ yuē duō wén quē yí shèn yán qí yú zé guǎ yóu

多见阙殆，慎行其余，则寡悔。”《为政2.18》
duō jiàn quē dài shèn xíng qí yǔ zé guǎ huǐ

Confucius said: "Listen more, reflect on what you hear, be careful with your speech; in this way, one will make less mistakes. Observe more, think about you see, pay attention to your actions; in this way, you will have less regrets." (On Governing 2.18)

Inspiration

We must be cautious about what we say and what we do whether we are officials or civilians. Always say and do only what is possible. Only thus can mistakes be minimized and regrettable things be prevented. This benefits both ourselves and the country.

子曰："君子欲讷于言而敏于行。"
zǐ yuē jūn zǐ yù nè yú yán ér mǐn yú xíng

《里仁4.24》

Confucius said: "A gentleman is slow to speak but prompt in action."
(On Virtue 4.24)

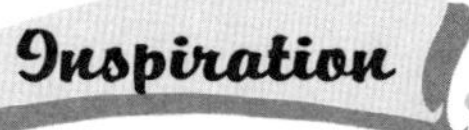

Less words, more action. Action speaks volumes.

子曰："暴虎冯河，死而无悔者，吾不与也。
zǐ yuē bào hǔ píng hé sǐ ér wú huǐ zhě wú bù yǔ yě

必也临事而惧，好谋而成者也。" 《述而7.11》
bì yě lín shì ér jù hào móu ér chéng zhě yě

Zi Lu asked: "Who would you appoint to direct the army?"
Confucius said: "I would not want to work with someone who has no fear of fighting a ferocious tiger or crossing a swelling river. I prefer someone who respects his assigned task and plans carefully before taking action."

(On Transmitting 7.11)

A foolhardy man cannot accomplish a great cause.

子曰：“文，莫吾犹人也。躬行君子，
zǐ yuē wén mò wú yóu rén yě gōng xíng jūn zǐ

则吾未之有得。” 《述而7.33》
zé wú wèi zhī yǒu dé

Confucius said: “In terms of knowledge, I am quite accomplished. But as to being a practising gentleman, I have yet to reach that stage.”
(On Transmitting 7.33)

Inspiration

Knowing is easy, doing is difficult. Even Confucius dared not say that he could always match his action with his words. His modesty and readiness to seek progress made him a highly respected figure.

子曰："诵《诗》三百，授之以政，不达；
zǐ yuē sòng shī sān bǎi shòu zhī yǐ zhèng bù dá

使于四方，不能专对；虽多，亦奚以为？"
shǐ yú sì fāng bù néng zhuān duì suī duō yì xī yǐ wéi

《子路13.5》

Confucius said: "Those who can recite the 300 poems in the *Book of Songs* but cannot run an administration effectively or handles diplomatic relationships independently have wasted their learning." (On Zi Lu 13.5)

Inspiration

Study does not simply mean stuffing our mind with book knowledge. It is important to put what we study into practice, contributing to our life and work.

子曰："工欲善其事，必先利其器。
zǐ yuē gōng yù shàn qí shì bì xiān lì qí qì

《卫灵公 15.10》

Confucius said: "If a craftsman wants to do a good job, he must first sharpen his tools." (On Duke Ling of Wei 15.10)

Inspiration

If you have no hand, you cannot make a fist. Without appropriate ingredients and kitchenware, you cannot cook despite your superior skills.

子曰：“吾尝终日不食，终夜不寝，以思，
zǐ yuē wú cháng zhōng rì bù shí zhōng yè bù qǐn yǐ sī

无益，不如学也。” 《卫灵公15.31》
wú yì bù rú xué yě

Confucius said: “I once tried to go without food for the whole day, and without sleep for the whole night, to meditate and think; but it produced little results. I should have spent that time studying instead.” (On Duke Ling of Wei 15.31)

Inspiration

Thinking, learning and practice are inseparable from one another. We need to strike a balance among them in order to achieve optimal results.

SELF-COMMUNITY RELATIONSHIP

A person cannot live all by himself. Therefore, it is important to maintain a good relationship between oneself and the community. When you do your job well and treat others honestly, you will have harmonious interpersonal relationships. If you live with a lame person, you will learn to limp. Therefore, the choice of our friends is very important to our growth and learning. "Do you and your friend have shared interests or pursuits? Are his deeds or words worth imitating?" We need to consider such factors.

子曰：“不患人之不己知，患不知人也。”
zǐ yuē bú huàn rén zhī bù jǐ zhī huàn bù zhī rén yě

《学而1.16》

Confucius said: "Do not worry about not being understood but be concerned about understanding others." (On Learning 1.16)

Inspiration

When we are not understood or even misunderstood, we may as well see it as an opportunity to cultivate our patience. In other words, we may take it as a test or training of moral cultivation.

子曰：“人而无信，不知其可也。大车无輗，
zǐ yuē rén ér wú xìn bù zhī qí kě yě dà chē wú ní

小车无軏，其何以行之哉？” 《为政2.22》
xiǎo chē wú yuè qí hé yǐ xíng zhī zāi

Confucius said: “If a person is not trustworthy, how can he establish himself? If a cart has no collar bar and a carriage has no yoke, how can they be made to move?” (On Governing 2.22)

Inspiration

A student asked Confucius how to make oneself accepted everywhere. Confucius told him, “If you are honest and modest in words and actions, you can certainly make yourself acceptable in foreign countries. On the contrary, if you fail to match your actions with your words, you will find yourself in an extremely difficult situation even in your homeland.”

子曰："主忠信，毋友不如己者，过则勿惮
zǐ yuē zhǔ zhōng xìn wú yǒu bù rú jǐ zhě guò zé wù dàn

改。" 《子罕9.25》
gǎi

Confucius said: "Value loyalty and trustworthiness above all. Do not make friends with those who have inferior values. When a mistake is made, do not be afraid of correcting it." (The Master Seldom 9.25)

Inspiration

Confucius had two disciples—Zi Xia and Zi Gong. Zi Xia liked to befriend those superior to him while Zi Gong liked to befriend those inferior to him. Confucius predicted that after he died, Zi Xia would make considerable progress while Zi Zong would not. Therefore, we need to be cautious in choosing the people we associate with.

曾子曰："君子以文会友，以友辅仁。"
zēng zǐ yuē jūn zǐ yǐ wén huì yǒu yǐ yǒu fǔ rén

《颜渊 12.24》

Zeng Zi said: "A gentleman makes friends by learning together with others, and he looks to friends to help him cultivate benevolence."
(On Yan Yuan 12.24)

Inspiration

If you and your friends spend time together drinking and eating, that is but a way of whiling away the days. Isn't it more enriching when you and your friends are able to motivate one another and add value to each other's lives by encouraging one another?

子路问曰：“何如斯可谓之士矣？”子曰：
zǐ lù wèn yuē hé rú sī kě wèi zhī shì yǐ zǐ yuē

“切切偲偲，怡怡如也，可谓士矣。
qiè qiè sī sī yí yí rú yě kě wèi shì yǐ

朋友切切偲偲，兄弟怡怡。”《子路13.28》
péng yǒu qiè qiè sī sī xiōng dì yí yí

Zi Lu asked: “How can one be known as a gentleman?
Confucius said: “One who encourages others and relates well with others can be called a gentleman. Friends should encourage each other and brothers should get along with one another.” (On Zi Lu 13.28)

Inspiration

When a person fails to act on what he says, the guidance of good knowledge or trustworthy friends will reduce the probability of him committing mistakes.

子曰：“君子矜而不争，群而不党。”
zǐ yuē jūn zǐ jīn ér bù zhēng qún ér bù dǎng

《卫灵公15.22》

Confucius said: "A gentleman is restrained and not contentious. He stresses harmonious living and not sectarianism." (On Duke Ling of Wei 15.22)

Inspiration

Although a gentleman leads a clean and honest life, he does not become narcissistic. He is different yet does not keep himself aloof from others. He tolerates and respects differing ideas, and gets along well with others.

子曰："君子无所争。必也射乎！揖让而升，
zǐ yuē jūn zǐ wú suǒ zhēng bì yě shè hū yī ràng ér shēng

下而饮。其争也君子。" 《八佾3.7》
xià ér yǐn qí zhēng yě jūn zǐ

Confucius said: "Among gentlemen, there is no contention. Even if there is rivalry, perhaps in archery. Before the contest, he bows to his rival, then he rises to compete. After the contest, he offers a toast to his rival. That is how gentlemen compete." (The Eight Rows 3.7)

Inspiration

Harmony is the key to the success of human relationship. A polite person will tend not to incur hatred and is popular.

孔子曰：“益者三友，损者三友。友直，
kǒng zǐ yuē yì zhě sān yǒu sǔn zhě sān yǒu yǒu zhí

友谅，友多闻，益矣。友便辟，友善柔，
yǒu liàng yǒu duō wén yì yǐ yǒu pián pì yǒu shàn róu

友便佞，损矣。” 《**季氏**16.4》
yǒu pián nìng sǔn yǐ

Confucius said: "There are three types of friendship that are beneficial and three kinds that are harmful. Friendship with the upright, the trustworthy, and the knowledgeable is beneficial. Friendship with the flattering, the insinuating and the braggart is harmful." (The Chief of the Ji Family 16.4)

Inspiration

An honest friend may not praise you. He may even say something that sounds rather harsh. Harsh as these honest words are, they are good for your growth.

朋友死，无所归，曰：“于我殡。”
péng yǒu sǐ　wú suǒ guī　yuē　yú wǒ bìn

《乡党10.22》

When a friend died and had no one to conduct the burial, Confucius said: "Let me arrange for the funeral." (When in the Village 10.22)

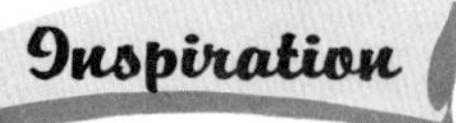

A true friend never abandon you in whatever circumstances.

子贡问友。子曰："忠告而善道之，不可则
zǐ gòng wèn yǒu　zǐ yuē　zhōng gào ér shàn dào zhī　bù kě zé

止，毋自辱焉。"　《颜渊12.23》
zhǐ　wú zì rǔ yān

Zi Gong asked about friendship. Confucius said: "Faithfully admonish your friends if they have done something wrong, and lead them gently to what is right. If they do not listen, do not go on. Don't humilate yourself."

(On Yan Yuan 12.23)

Inspiration

It is our duty to admonish our friends when their actions deviate from rules and laws. However, good advice is harsh to the ear. Not everyone accepts good advice, we can only do our best.

子曰：“爱之，能勿劳乎？忠焉，能勿诲乎？”
zǐ yuē ài zhī néng wù láo hū zhōng yān néng wù huì hū

《宪问14.7》

Confucius said: "If you love a person, how can you not encourage him to work hard? If you are loyal to a person, how can you not tell him when he is doing wrong?" (Xian Questions 14.7)

Inspiration

Deep love needs to be coupled with high responsibility. Loving and staying faithful to a person do not mean complete conformity. Accommodation, doting, and passive loyalty can do harm to the person you love.

子曰：“众恶之，必察焉；众好之，必察焉。”
zǐ yuē zhòng wù zhī bì chá yān zhòng hào zhī bì chá yān

《卫灵公15.28》

Confucius said: "When a person is unpopular, it is necessary to find out why that is so. When a person is popular, it is also necessary to find out why."
(On Duke Ling of Wei 15.28)

Inspiration

We should not only consider a single aspect when assessing a person or a thing. Nor should we only echo what others say. We need to observe carefully before coming to any conclusion.

子曰：“视其所以，观其所由，察其所安，
zǐ yuē shì qí suǒ yǐ guān qí suǒ yóu chá qí suǒ ān

人焉廋哉！人焉廋哉！” 《为政2.10》
rén yān sōu zāi rén yān sōu zāi

Confucius said: "We can know a person by observing his behaviour, understanding the reasons for his actions and ascertaining his intentions. If we do this, how can we not know him?" (On Governing 2.10)

Inspiration

We tend to judge a person by his words and action. Confucius did not do this. He always made a point to observe a person from different perspectives. This is a sign of respect.

子曰："唯仁者，能好人，能恶人。"
zǐ yuē wéi rén zhě néng hào rén néng wù rén

《里仁4.3》

Confucius said: "Only a virtuous man can discern accurately who is good, and who is evil." (On Virtue 4.3)

Inspiration

Your mood plays a part in determining whether you like or hate a person. A gentleman does not allow his emotions to cloud his judgement. This enables him to conduct a correct and fair assessment of a person.

宰予昼寝。子曰：“朽木不可雕也，粪土之墙不可圬也。
zǎi yǔ zhòu qǐn zǐ yuē xiǔ mù bù kě diāo yě fèn tǔ zhī qiáng bù kě wū yě

于予与何诛？”子曰：“始吾于人也，听其言而信其行；
yú yú yú hé zhū zǐ yuē shǐ wú yú rén yě tīng qí yán ěr xìn qí xíng

今吾于人也，听其言而观其行。于予与改是。”
jīn wú yú rén yě tīng qí yán ér guān qí xíng yú yú yú gǎi shì

《公冶长5. 10》

Zai Xu was found sleeping in the day. Confucius said: “Rotten wood cannot be carved, nor a soiled wall be whitewashed. What is the use of rebuking someone like Zai Yu?” He continued: “I used to believe that men practised what they said. But now, I will measure a person’s words against his actions before I believe his claims. My views have changed because of Zai Yu.”

(On Gong Ye Zhang 5.10)

Inspiration

Words can cheat. Yet, daily behaviour easily reveals one’s level of moral cultivation.

互乡难与言，童子见*，门人惑，子曰："与其进
hù xiāng nán yǔ yán tóng zǐ xiàn mén rén huò zǐ yuē yǔ qí jìn

也，不与其退也，唯何甚？人洁己以进，与其洁
yě bù yǔ qí tuì yě wéi hé shèn rén jié jǐ yǐ jìn yǔ qí jié

也，不保其往也。" 《述而7.29》
yě bù bǎo qí wǎng yě

Hu village was a barbaric region. To his disciples' surprise, Confucius accepted a disciple from the Hu tribe. Confucius said: "I support their progress but reject their barbaric ways. Since he came with the intention of improving himself, we should support him rather than be too hard on him and keep harping on his past." (On Transmitting 7.29)

Inspiration

Learning from others' merits and being tolerant of their demerits not only make us more broad-minded, but also help us get along well with others.

*见：同"现"。

子曰："论笃是与，君子者乎？色庄者乎？"
zǐ yuē lùn dǔ shì yǔ jūn zǐ zhě hū sè zhuāng zhě hū

《先进 11.21》

Confucius said: "A person may earnestly promote honesty verbally, but how can one know if he is truly a gentleman, or just a pretence?"
(On the Forerunners 11.21)

Inspiration

A hypocrite talks about virtues and morality in the presence of others, but does something totally different when he is alone. To tell a true gentleman from a hypocrite, we need to "listen to what he says and watch what he does". A gentleman means what he says.

阙党童子将命。或问之曰：“益者与？”
quē dǎng tōng zǐ jiāng mìng huò wèn zhī yuē yì zhě yú

子曰：“吾见其居于位也，见其与先生并行也。
zǐ yuē wú jiàn qí jū yú wèi yě jiàn qí yǔ xiān shēng bìng xíng yě

非求益者也，欲速成者也。” 《宪问14.44》
fēi qiú yì zhě yě yù sù chéng zhě yě

A boy from Que village came to see Confucius. Someone asked Confucius: "Does this boy strive for progress?" Confucius said: "I observed that he wants to sit in prominent positions and walk among learned elders. He is not one who strives for progress, but one who is impatient for success."

(Xian Questions 14.44)

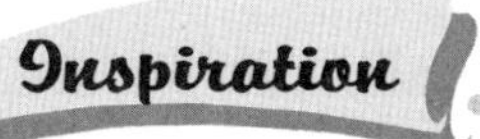

A person's behaviour or his body language reflects his character and heart.

子曰：“可与言，而不与之言，失人；不可与言，
zǐ yuē kě yǔ yán ér bù yǔ zhī yán shī rén bù kě yǔ yán

而与之言，失言。知* 者不失人，亦不失言。”
ér yǔ zhī yán shī yán zhì zhě bù shī rén yì bù shī yán

《卫灵公15.8》

Confucius said: “Not speaking to one who is worthy to be spoken to is to have missed a great opportunity. Speaking to one who is not worthy to be spoken to is to have wasted your words. A wise man does not let a worthy man slip by or waste his words.” (On Duke Ling of Wei 15.8)

Inspiration

We cannot forgo interpersonal communication in life. Yet, we need to develop the ability to identify who will make good friends and who are nodding acquaintances.

*知：同“智”。

子曰："吾之于人也，谁毁谁誉？如有所誉者，
zǐ yuē wú zhī yú rén yě shuí huǐ shuí yù rú yǒu suǒ yù zhě

其有所试矣。斯民也，三代之所以直道而行也。"
qí yǒu suǒ shì yǐ sī mín yě sān dài zhī suǒ yǐ zhí dào ér xíng yě

《卫灵公15.25》

Confucius said: "Towards others, I do not lightly criticise or give praise. If I praise someone, it is because his deeds had been proven. Men of three dynasties have done the same, and that has kept them on the right path."
Note: The three dynasties refer to Xia, Shang and Zhou.

(On Duke Ling of Wei 15.25)

I don't slander or praise others for no reason.

Inspiration

Words are like a sharp weapon. Not used properly, they may hurt. We should be responsible for what we say and refrain from saying anything that cannot stand the test.

子贡曰：“君子亦有恶乎？”子曰：“有恶：
zǐ gòng yuē jūn zǐ yì yǒu wù hū zǐ yuē yǒu wù

恶称人之恶者，恶居下（流）而讪上者，恶勇而
wù chēng rén zhī è zhě wù jū xià liú ér shàn shàng zhě wù yǒng ér

无礼者，恶果敢而窒者。” 《阳货17.24》
wú lǐ zhě wù guǒ gǎn ér zhì zhě

Zi Gong asked: “Is there anything that a gentleman hates?
Confucius said: “Yes, there are. A gentleman abhors those who malign others, despises those who slander their superiors, detests those who have courage but lack graciousness, and dislikes those who are rash but obstinate.”
(On Yang Huo 17.24)

A gentleman is not a yes-man. He also hates unprincipled men and unjust things. This is what the sense of justice means.

THE WORTH OF LIFE

Ancient Greek philosopher Heraclitus once said that a man cannot step twice into the same river ("Upon those who step into the 'same river', different and ever different waters flow down."). The reason is that the river is flowing; the river you step into at this moment will be different from what you walked into a moment ago. Time flows nonstop, independent of everyone's will. Despite today's considerable advances in science and technology, death remains an unsolved mystery. Primarily because we do not know exactly what death is, we need to seize every opportunity and live life to the fullest.

子贡曰："贫而无谄，富而无骄，何如？"
zǐ gòng yuē pín ér wú chǎn fù ér wú jiāo hé rú

子曰："可也。未若贫而乐，富而好礼者也。"
zǐ yuē kě yě wèi ruò pín ér lè fù ér hào lǐ zhě yě

《学而1.15》

Zi Gong asked: "What do you think of a person who is poor but does not flatter the rich, or who is rich but is not haughty?"
Confucius said: "That is good. But better still is a person who is poor but joyful, or rich and yet gracious." (On Learning 1.15)

Inspiration

Poverty and wealth are external material conditions. Getting or losing them does not affect our inherent worth. To be content in all circumstances is to be wealthy indeed.

子曰："贫而无怨难，富而无骄易。"
zǐ yuē pín ér wú yuàn nán fù ér wú jiāo yì

《子路14.10》

Confucius said: "To be poor and not complain—that is hard. To be rich and not proud—that is relatively easier." (Xian Questions 14.10)

Inspiration

Wealth and rank are what everybody aspires for while poverty is what everybody wants to escape from. It is not easy at all to keep your mind unaffected by physical circumstances.

子曰：“富与贵，是人之所欲也，不以其道得之，
zǐ yuē fù yǔ guì shì rén zhī suǒ yù yě bù yǐ qí dào dé zhī

不处也。贫与贱，是人之所恶也，不以其道得之，
bù chǔ yě pín yǔ jiàn shì rén zhī suǒ wù yě bù yǐ qí dào dé zhī

不去也。《里仁4.5》
bù qù yě

Confucius said:"Everyone wants to be rich and powerful. But it is better not to attain it than to use unscrupulous means to acquire it. No one wants to be poor and despised. But it is better not to be free from it than to use dishonest means to escape from it." (On Virtue 4.5)

Inspiration

Confucius did not think of himself as a lofty and upright man who regarded wealth as dirt. He admitted that it is natural to desire wealth. Once, he said that if doing a lowly job which required him to use a whip would get him rich, he is willing to do it. However, he would rather do what he loved if richness had to be acquired by wrong means.

子曰："贤哉，回也！一箪食，一瓢饮，
zǐ yuē xián zāi huí yě yī dān shí yī piáo yǐn

在陋巷，人不堪其忧，回也不改其乐。
zài lòu xiàng rén bù kān qí yōu huí yě bù gǎi qí lè

贤哉，回也！"《雍也6.11》
xián zāi huí yě

Confucius said: "How virtuous Yan Hui is! A simple bowl of rice, a plain cup of water, living in a shabby hut—most men would not be able to withstand such misery, but Yan Hui manages to remain so joyful. How virtuous Yan Hui is!" (About Yong Ye 6.11)

Inspiration

Yan Hui was one of Confucius' favourite students. Confucius once said: "Yan Hui can concentrate his mind on the theory of benevolence for a long time. In contrast, other students can only think of it occassionally." Unfortunately, Yan Hui was feeble and died young. Confucius wept, "O Heaven, you are taking my life away! You are taking my life away!"

子曰：“饭疏食饮水，曲肱而枕之，乐亦
zǐ yuē fàn shū shí yǐn shuǐ qū gōng ér zhěn zhī lè yì

在其中矣。不义而富且贵，于我如浮云。”
zài qí zhōng yǐ bù yì ér fù qiě guì yú wǒ rú fú yún

《述而7.16》

Confucius said: “Having a simple meal, propping up on my arms for a nap, joy can be found in such. Ill-gotten riches are to me just as clouds passing in the sky.”
(On Transmitting 7.16)

Inspiration

Happiness cannot be measured by material wealth. A poor man can also lead a happy life. There was once a Western sage by the name of Diogenes whose personal belongings consisted of an olive branch, a shabby robe, a food bag and a blanket. He slept in a wine barrel by night. He enjoyed himself despite this poverty-stricken condition.

子曰：“君子谋道不谋食。耕也，馁在其中矣；
zǐ yuē jūn zǐ móu dào bù móu shí gēng yě něi zài qí zhōng yǐ

学也，禄在其中矣。君子忧道不忧贫。”
xué yě lù zài qí zhōng yǐ jūn zǐ yōu dào bù yōu pín

《卫灵公15.32》

Confucius said: “A gentleman seeks the Way above seeking food. In farming, we may sometimes go hungry; in learning, one may receive an official salary. A gentleman is concerned about the Way and not about poverty.”
(On Duke Ling of Wei 15.32)

Inspiration

A man who has discovered the worth of his life will have nothing to lose in this world. That is why a gentleman can live in poverty while at the same time keeping his moral integirty. Honour or disgrace, loss or gain, all these factors cannot alter his inherent worth.

子曰："知*者乐水，仁者乐山。知*者动，
zǐ yuē zhì zhě lè shuǐ rén zhě lè shān zhì zhě dòng

仁者静。知*者乐，仁者寿。"《雍也6.23》
rén zhě jìng zhì zhě lè rén zhě shòu

Confucius says: "The wise delights in flowing waters; the benevolent delights in majestic mountains. The wise is active; the benevolent is restful. The wise enjoys life; the benevolent enjoys longevity." (About Yong Ye 6.23)

Inspiration

Running water is never stale. An intelligent man is as flexible as the running water, and he is full of vitality. A benevolent man, who takes benevolence as the essence of his life, will remain solid and firm as a rock in whatever circumstances.

*知：智

子曰：“人无远虑，必有近忧。”
zǐ yuē rén wú yuǎn lǜ bì yǒu jìn yōu

《卫灵公15.12》

Confucius said: “One without long term plans will be troubled by worries close at hand.” (On Duke Ling of Wei 15.12)

Inspiration

A life not well organised will make one ill-prepared for both the present and the future.

子曰："吾十有*五而志于学，三十而立，
zǐ yuē wǔ shí yǒu wǔ ér zhì yú xué sān shí ér lì

四十而不惑，五十而知天命，六十而耳顺，
sì shí ér bù huò wǔ shí ér zhī tiān mìng liù shí ér ěr shùn

七十而从心所欲，不逾距。" 《为政2.4》
qī shí ér cóng xīn suǒ yù bù yú jǔ

Confucius said: "At fifteen, I set my mind to acquire knowledge. At thirty, I establish my foundation. At forty, I learnt to manage perplexities. At fifty, I came to understand heaven's will for me. At sixty, I was able to decern the truth in others' words. At seventy, I could follow my heart's desires without transgressing what is right." (On Governing 2.4)

Inspiration

Life is a process of continuous effort to make progress. A stagnant or futile life is lamentable.

*有：又。

子曰："朝闻道，夕死可矣！"　《里仁4.8》
zǐ yuē　zhāo wén dào　xī sǐ kě yǐ

Confucius said: "If I hear and grasp the truth in the morning, and die in the evening, I will have no regrets." (On Virtue 4.8)

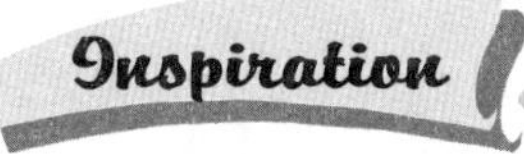

Life is valuable indeed. Yet death is nothing horrible when the truth of life and universe is grasped.

子路曰："愿闻子之志。"子曰："老者安
zǐ lù yuē yuàn wén zǐ zhī zhì zǐ yuē lǎo zhě ān

之，朋友信之，少者怀之。" 《公冶长5.26》
zhī péng yǒu xìn zhī shào zhě huái zhī

Zi Lu asked Confucius: "Teacher, we would like to know what are your aspirations."
Confucius replied: "I hope to see the aged enjoy peace, there is trust among friends and the young being cared for." (On Gong Ye Zhang 5.26)

Inspiration

We should have a wider vision. We should be concerned about both ourselves and the society at large. Only thus can we have a more meaningful life.

子曰：“志于道，据于德，依于仁，游于艺。”

zǐ yuē zhì yú dào jù yú dé yī yú rén yóu yú yì

《述而7.6》

Confucius said: “A man should set his sight on the Way, base his conduct on virtue, be guided by benevolence in living, and take recreation in the arts.” Note: The six arts refer to rites, music, archery, chariot-riding, literature and mathematics.

(On Transmitting 7.6)

Inspiration

After a man settles down and gets on with his pursuit, he will no longer be like a rootless duckweed drifting here and there with nothing to depend on.

子在川上，曰：“逝者如斯夫！不舍昼夜。”
zǐ zài chuān shàng yuē shì zhě rú sī fú bù shě zhòu yè

《子罕9.17》

Confucius stood beside a stream and said: “Time is like a river, flowing away endlessly day and night.” (The Master Seldom 9.17)

Inspiration

Ancient Greek philosopher Heraclitus once said that a man cannot step twice into the same river. The reason is that the river is flowing—the river you step into at this moment will be different from what you walked into a moment ago. Time flows nonstop, independent of everyone's will.

子不语怪、力、乱、神。 《述而7.21》

zǐ bù yǔ guài lì luàn shén

Confucius never spoke about monsters, feats of strength, violence and disorders, the paranormal and spirits. (On Transmitting 7.21)

Inspiration

We do not know much about what happens around us, let alone the fabricated supernatural things, feats of strength, disorders and spiritual beings. We should be grounded in reality rather than give ourselves to whims and fantasy. Only thus can we keep our attention focused on what is important.

季路问事鬼神。子曰：“未能事人，焉能事鬼？”
jì lù wèn shì guǐ shén zǐ yuē wèi néng shì rén yān néng shì guǐ

曰：“敢问死？”曰：“未知生，焉知死？”
yuē gǎn wèn sǐ yuē wèi zhī shēng yān zhī sǐ

《先进11.12》

Ji Lu asked about serving the spirits of the dead and the gods. Confucius said: "You do not even know how to serve man, how can you serve the spirits?"
Ji Lu said: "May I then ask about death?"
Confucius answered: "You do not even understand life, how can you understand death?" (On the Forerunners 11.12)

Inspiration

In spite of outstanding advances made in science and technologies today, death remains a mystery to many. We cannot figure out exactly what death is like. But we are sure of one thing: You will surely regret when you die if you have not made full use of your life.

鸟之将死，其鸣也哀；人之将死，其言也善。
niǎo zhī jiāng sǐ qí míng yě āi rén zhī jiāng sǐ qí yán yě shàn

《泰伯8.4》

When a bird is dying, its cry is sorrowful; when a man is dying, his words are kind. (On Tai Bo 8.4)

Inspiration

It is too late to regret at the last moment of our life. We need to get along well with others and do as many worthwhile things as possible while we can.

子曰：“凤鸟不至，河不出图，吾已矣夫！”
zǐ yuē fèng niǎo bú zhì hé bù chū tú wú yǐ yǐ fú

《子罕9.9》

Confucius said: "Without the appearance of the phoenix and the Yellow River Octogram, there is no hope for an enlightened government, and no hope for me."
Note: According to legend, the phoenix is a sign of blessing, as well as the uprightness of the government. And as for the Yellow River Octogram which is carried on the back of a dragon-horse, it is a sign that precedes the birth of a sage who would bring salvation to the world.(The Master Seldom 9.9)

A benevolent man holds himself responsible for the world. He becomes worried before anyone else and enjoys life only after everyone else finds enjoyment.

子曰："不怨天，不尤人，下学而上达。
zǐ yuē bù yuàn tiān bù yóu rén xià xué ér shàng dá

知我者其天乎！" 《宪问14.35》
zhī wǒ zhě qí tiān hū

Confucius said: "Even if no one understands me, I will not blame heaven or man, for I received my enlightenment by learning from everyday matters. Perhaps only heaven understands me!" (Xian Questions 14.35)

Inspiration

We often complain when we encounter unpleasant things. However, we should not always blame our unhappy experience on heaven and others. Otherwise, nobody would like us. It is hard to change the circumstances, but it is possible to change our way of thinking.

子曰：“人能弘道，非道弘人。”
zǐ yuē rén néng hóng dào fēi dào hóng rén

《卫灵公15.29》

Confucius said: “It is man who elevates the Way. The Way is not used to elevate man.” (On Duke Ling of Wei 15.29)

Inspiration

Principles are inanimate and they become useful only when they are put into practice.

LIFE AND ART

Confucius took an earnest attitude towards life. He had a very regular habit of work and rest. He attached great importance to drinking and eating. For instance, he did not speak while having food; he did not eat until the eating hour; he did not eat excessively; he did not speak before going to bed; and he could always keep the right sleeping posture. All these are very good living habits. Confucius was fond of the arts, such as listening to music and reading the *Book of Songs.* He believed that the arts were conducive to one's moral cultivation.

林放问礼之本。子曰："大哉问！礼，与其奢也，
lín fàng wèn lǐ zhī běn zǐ yuē dà zāi wèn lǐ yǔ qí shē yě

宁俭；丧，与其易也，宁戚。"《八佾 3.4》
nìng jiǎn sāng yǔ qí yì yě nìng qī

Lin Fang asked Confucius what the key essence of rites is. Confucius replied: "That is a big question! Let's say we talk about a ceremonial rite; it is better to keep it simple than to be extravagant. Or if we look at a funeral rite; heartfelt grief is more important than grand rituals." (The Eight Rows 3.4)

Inspiration

Rites and rituals, if not based on true sentiments, are nothing but empty formalities.

子于是日哭，则不歌。《述而7.10》

zǐ yú shì rì kū zé bù gē

On a day when Confucius wept at a funeral, he would not sing.

(On Transmitting 7.10)

Inspiration

A sage like Confucius also cries. When his beloved student Yan Hui died, Confucius cried in great sorrow, "Oh, heaven, take me away! Take me away!" Confucius also hummed a song when in high spirits. Whether he wept or sang, he was expressing his true and sincere feelings. Emotions lend richness to life.

子之燕*居，申申如也，夭夭如也。
zǐ zhī yàn jū shēn shēn rú yě yāo yāo rú yě

《述而7.4》

When Confucius was at home, he always made himself look neat, and was relaxed and cheerful. (On Transmitting 7.4)

Inspiration

Greek philosopher Democritus said: "Even if you are alone, you should not malign others or commit misdeeds. You should develop a keener sense of shame when you are by yourself."

*燕：同"宴"。

食不厌精，脍不厌细。 《乡党10.8》
shí bú yàn jīng kuài bú yàn xì

In grinding grain, the finer the better. In slicing meat, the thinner the better.
(When in the Village 10.8)

Confucius's meticulous views on eating reveal his serious life attitude. Such an attitude also indicates his effort to treasure his own life.

食不语，寝不言。 《乡党10.10》
shí bù yǔ qǐn bù yán

Do not speak when eating; do not talk while sleeping.
(When in the Village 10.10)

Inspiration

A man asks a Zen Buddhist master: "How do you cultivate yourself?" The master replies: "Eat when I am hungry, and sleep when I am tired." The man says: "Is not everybody doing this? Can this also be called cultivation?" The master answers: "Usually a man keeps his mind occupied with various desires when eating; and weighing the pros and cons while lying in bed."

席不正，不坐。 《乡党10. 12》

xí bú zhèng bú zuò

If the sitting mat is not laid according to the rituals, do not sit on it.
Note: In ancient times, at a feast, everyone was given a mat to sit on. There were many rules surrounding the use of these mats, for example, the host's mat must always face east. (When in the Village 10.12)

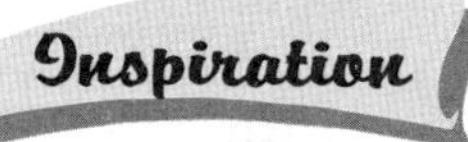

A principled man is better than a man of no principles.

乡人饮酒，杖者出，斯出矣。 《乡党10.13》

xiāng rén yǐn jiǔ zhàng zhě chū sī chū yǐ

When drinking with fellow villagers, do not leave until the elders had done so.
(When in the Village 10.13)

Inspiration

Respecting the elderly is a fundamental part of the ethics. Leaving after the elderly, giving seats to the elderly and other such daily acts are a barometer of our moral integrity.

寝不尸，居不客。 **《乡党**10.24》

qǐn bù shī jū bú kè

When sleeping, never lie supine like a corpse. When living at home, there is no need to be solemn like at a ceremony or when one is receiving guests.
(When in the Village 10.24)

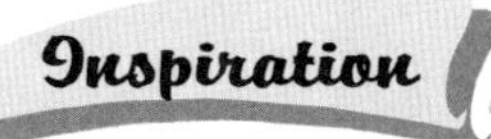

Sleeping and seating require different appropriate postures. Constant watch over our own behaviour is a form of self-awareness.

升车，必正立，执绥。车中，不内顾，不疾
shēng chē bì zhèng lì zhí suí chē zhōng bú nèi gù bù jí

言，不亲指。《乡党10.26》
yán bù qīn zhǐ

Before boarding the carriage, stand upright and hold the carriage band for support to ascend. In the carriage, do not peer around, speak loudly or point with your finger. (When in the Village 10.26)

Inspiration

We do not pay much attention to our daily behaviour. Confucius' elaborate dos and don'ts may sound ridiculous to us. Actually, paying attention to our words and action is a way of respecting ourselves and others.

（曾皙）曰："莫* 春者，春服既成，冠者五
zēng xī yuē mù chūn zhě chūn fú jì chéng guàn zhě wǔ

六人，童子六七人，浴乎沂，风乎舞雩，咏
liù rén tóng zǐ liù qī rén yù hū yí fēng hū wǔ yú yǒng

而归。"
ér guī

《先进11. 26》

Zeng Xi said: "My aspiration is to go for an outing in late spring. Wearing my spring clothes, joining some youths and children, we would go swimming in the Yi River, sunbathing in the gentle breeze on the Rain Altar, and end with singing together on the way home." (On the Forerunners 11.26)

Inspiration

While working hard in our daily life, we also need a breather from time to time. Let us take a walk in the breeze, sing freely or have a good time with our families or friends. This will create for us a balanced and joyful life.

*莫：同"暮"。

子所雅言，《诗》、《书》、执礼，皆雅言也。
zǐ suǒ yǎ yán shī shū zhí lǐ jiē yǎ yán yě

《述而7.18》

When Confucius recited the *Book of Songs*, taught the *Book of History* and administered the rites, he will speak with the correct pronunication instead of in his Lu dialect. (On Transmitting 7.18)

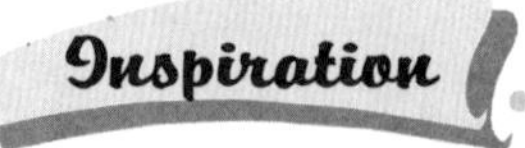

It is an art and also a courteous act to know what language to speak in what situation.

子曰：“小子何莫学夫《诗》？《诗》，可以兴，
zǐ yuē xiǎo zǐ hé mò xué fū shī shī kě yǐ xīng

可以观，可以群，可以怨。迩之事父，远之事君，
kě yǐ guān kě yǐ qún kě yǐ yuàn ěr zhī shì fù yuǎn zhī shì jūn

多识于鸟兽草木之名！” 《阳货17.9》
duō shì yú niǎo shòu cǎo mù zhī míng

Confucius said: "My students, why didn't you study the *Book of Songs*? The *Book of Songs* can stimulate your passions, enhance your cultural understanding, develop in you a heart for relations, and help you in expressing lamentations. An immediate result is that it helps one serve one's parents well. The far-reaching effect is that it can help one serve one's ruler well. It can even acquaint one with the names of birds, animals and plants."

(On Yang Huo 17.9)

Inspiration

China's first poetry anthology, the *Book of Songs* is a collection of poems. The book consists of three parts—"*feng* (folksongs)", "*ya* (songs performed at banquets given by the imperial court or noble houses during the Zhou Dynasty)" and "*song* (songs chanted during sacrificial activities at ancestral temples)".

子夏问曰：“‘巧笑倩兮，美目盼兮，素以为绚兮。’
zǐ xià wèn yuē qiǎo xiào qiànxī měi mù pàn xī sù yǐ wéi xuàn xī

何谓也？”子曰：“绘事后素。”曰：“礼后乎？”
hé wèi yě zǐ yuē huì shì hòu sù yuē lǐ hòu hū

子曰：“起予者商也，始可与言《诗》已矣。”
zǐ yuē qǐ yú zhě shāng yě shǐ kě yǔ yán shī yǐ yǐ

《八佾3.8》

Zi Xia asked Confucius: “A captivating smile, beautiful eyes, just like flowers drawn on a white background. What does these verses of the poem mean?”
Confucius replied: “In painting, the subject is always drawn on a white background.”
Zi Xia said: “Can I interpret this verse to mean that customs are built on benevolence as a foundation?”
Overjoyed with Zi Xia's insight, Confucius said: “The ability to interpret the verse in this way shows that you are ready to discuss the *Book of Songs* with me.”
(The Eight Rows 3.8)

Inspiration

At birth, we are just like a blank sheet of paper. The surroundings in which we grow up, and the habits we have developed are comparable to the different colours printed on the paper, resulting in thousands of different human personalities.

子谓《韶》："尽美矣，又尽善也。"谓
zǐ wèi sháo jìn měi yǐ yòu jìn shàn yě wèi

《武》："尽美矣，未尽善也。"《八佾3.25》
wǔ jìn měi yǐ wèi jìn shàn yě

Confucius praised Shao music saying: "Its form and contents are both good." But as to Wu music, he said: "Although its form is beautiful, its content leaves a person in want." (The Eight Rows 3.25)

Inspiration

A literary work should be assessed not only by its external form but also by its content. We need to see if its content conforms to certain important norms.

子曰："兴于《诗》，立于礼，成于乐。"
zǐ yuē xīng yú shī lì yú lǐ chéng yú yuè

《泰伯8.8》

Confucius said: "The *Book of Songs* inspires me, the rites provide me with principles to live by, and music grants me fulfillment." (On Tai Bo 8.8)

Without feelings and ideals, life will be dull and flat.

子曰："《诗》三百，一言以蔽之，曰：思无邪。"
zǐ yuē shī sān bǎi yì yán yǐ bì zhī yuē sī wú xié

《为政2.2》

Confucius said: "The *Book of Songs* contains three hundred entries. If I have to summarise the teaching of the book in one phrase, it would be 'a pure and untainted mind'." (On Governing 2.2)

Inspiration

It is good to form a reading habit. Yet, it is also important to know what is worth reading and what needs to cast aside. Morally correct content will uplift our lives while an immoral one will lead us astray.

子曰：“《关雎》，乐而不淫，哀而不伤。”
zǐ yuē guān jū lè ér bù yín āi ér bù shāng

《八佾 3. 20》

Confucius said: "The poem 'Guan Sui' is joyous but not licentious, melancholic but not depressing." (The Eight Rows 3.20)

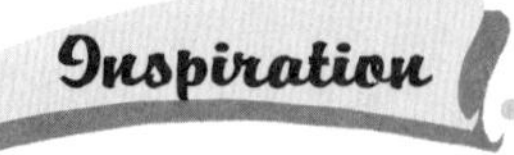

Extreme or violent emotions hurt both yourself and others. Letting loose your emotions is a sign of a lack in self-restraint.

子在齐闻《韶》，三月不知肉味。 曰：
zǐ zài qí wén shāo sān yuè bù zhī ròu wèi yuē

"不图为乐之至于斯也！" 《述而7.14》
bù tú wéi yuè zhī zhì yú sī yě

Confucius heard Shao music performed in the state of Qi. For three months, he found meat tastless. He said: "I never thought I would become be so lost in music to reach this state." (On Transmitting 7.14)

Inspiration

No matter what you do, be it reading or listening to music, when you devote your heart and soul to it, you will derive great delight.

子谓伯鱼曰："女为《周南》、《召南》矣乎？
zǐ wèi bó yú yuē rǔ wéi zhōu nán zhào nán yǐ hū

人而不为《周南》、《召南》，其犹正墙面而立
rén ér bù wéi zhōu nán zhào nán qí yóu zhèng qiáng miàn ér lì

也与？"
yě yú

《阳货17.10》

Confucius said to his son Bo Yu: "Have you studied the *Zhou Nan* and the *Zhao Nan*?" A person who has not studied the *Zhou Nan* and the *Zhao Nan* is like one standing with his face against a wall." (On Yang Huo 17.10)

Inspiration

Good literary and artistic works are not only entertaining but also instructive. They nourish our lives, help us go forward and elevate our minds.

Index

Ren 仁

Chapter	Pg no.	Translation
On Yang Huo 17.8	42	Those who love benevolence but not...
On Virtue 4.1	54	The excellence of a neighbourhood is in its...
On Virtue 4.2	55	A man without virtue cannot endure...
About Yong Ye 6.30	57	A benevolent person is one who helps...
On Transmitting 7.30	58	Is benevolence very far from us? If we truly...
On Yan Yuan 12.1	60	To be able to overcome your desire and...
On Yan Yuan 12.22	61	Fan Chi asked:"What is benevolence?"...
Xian Questions 14.4	62	A benevolent man is courageous, but those...
On Yang Huo 17.17	65	Those with flattering lips and who pretend...
On Learning 1.2	66	Filial piety and fraternal respect—these are...
On Tai Bo 8.7	85	A learned man must make it his...
The Master Seldom 9.29	89	The wise is never confused. The...
On Duke Ling of Wei 15.9	91	A righteous man would not compromise benevolence because he fears death, but...
On Duke Ling of Wei 15.36	92	When the occasion calls for practising...
On Yan Yuan 12.24	139	A gentleman makes friends by learning...
On Virtue 4.3	149	Only a virtuous man can discern accurately...
About Yong Ye 6.23	164	The wise delights in flowing waters; the benevolent delights in majestic mountains. The wise is active; the benevolent is restful. The wise enjoys life; the benevolent enjoys...
On Transmitting 7.6	169	A man should set his sight on the Way...

Yi 义

Chapter	Pg no.	Translation
On Virtue 4.16	75	The gentleman considers...
On Duke Ling of Wei 15.18	80	When one abides by righteousness...
The Chief of the Ji Family 16.10	81	...does he ponder whether he deserves...
On Zi Zhang 19.1	94	A learned man, in the face of danger, is...
On Duke Ling of Wei 15.17	113	Those who gather for small talk all day...
On Transmitting 7.16	162	Ill-gotten riches are to me just as clouds...

Li 礼

Chapter	Pg no.	Translation
On Yan Yuan 12.1	60	To be able to overcome your desire and observe the rites in living; this is benevolence.
On Yan Yuan 12.5	72	If a gentleman is excellent in his work, does...
On Duke Ling of Wei 15.18	80	When one abides by righteousness as a...
On Tai Bo 8.2	110	Courtesy without following the rites leads to weariness. Being overly cautious without...
On Governing 2.3	117	If people are inspired by a moral and...
On Zi Lu 13.3	124	...If work does not get done, then music and the rites cannot be implemented. If music and the rites are...
On Yang Huo 17.24	156	...detests those who have courage but lack...
On Learning 1.15	158	...But better still is a person who is poor but...
The Eight Rows 3.4	178	Lin Fang asked Confucius what the key...
On Transmitting 7.18	188	When Confucius recited the *Book of Songs*, taught the *Book of History* and administered the rites, he will speak with the correct...
The Eight Rows 3.8	190	...Can I interpret this verse to mean that...
On Tai Bo 8.8	192	The *Book of Songs* inspires me, the rites provide me with principles to live by, and...

Zhi 知

Xin 信

Chapter	Pg no.	Translation
On Yang Huo 17.8	42	Those who love honesty but not learning...
On Transmitting 7.25	48	Confucius educated his students in four...
On Duke Ling of Wei 15.18	80	... speaks with modesty and is trustworthy...
On Learning 1.4	96	...Have I been trustworthy in my...
On Yan Yuan 12.7	120	Without the people's trust, the government...
On Governing 2.22	137	If a person is not trustworthy, how can he...
The Master Seldom 9.25	138	Value loyalty and trustworthiness above all...
On Gong Ye Zhang 5.10	150	I used to believe that men practised what...

Zhong 忠

Chapter	Pg no.	Translation
On Transmitting 7.25	48	Confucius educated his students in four...
On Learning 1.4	96	Zeng Zi said: "Daily, I examine myself in three areas. Have I done my best when doing...
The Master Seldom 9.25	138	Confucius said: "Value loyalty and trustworthiness above all. Do not make friends with those who have inferior values...
On Yan Yuan 12.23	145	Zi Gong asked about friendship. Confucius said: "Faithfully admonish your friends if they have done something wrong, and lead them gently to what is right...
Xian Questions 14.7	146	Confucius said: "If you love a person, how can you not encourage him to work hard? If you are loyal to a person, how can you not tell him when he is doing...

Xiao 孝

Chapter	Pg no.	Translation
On Learning 1.2	66	You Zi said: "A man who is filial to his parents and respects his elder brothers is seldom disposed to rebel against the authorities. He who is not disposed to rebel against the authorities will not be disposed to stir up chaos and create confusion. The gentleman devotes his attention to building the foundation of life. When this is firmly established, the Way is naturally conceived. Filial piety and fraternal respect—these are indeed the foundation and the roots of virtue and benevolence!"
On Learning 1.11	67	Confucius said: "When a man's father is alive, check his aspirations. When a man's father is deceased, observe his conduct. If he did not waver from the promises made and principles taught by his father after three years of his father's death, he can be said to be a filial son."
On Governing 2.7	68	Zi You consulted Confucius about filial piety. Confucius said: "These days, meeting the physical needs of parents is considered filial piety. But even dogs and horses are likewise cared for. What difference is there if one does not show his parents respect?"

Zheng 正

Chapter	Pg no.	Translation
On Yan Yuan 12.17	122	When Ji Kang Zi asked Confucius how one should govern, Confucius answered: "To govern means to be upright. If you lead the people in an upright way, who will dare to be corrupt?"
On Zi Lu 13.6	123	Confucius said: "If the ruler is upright, even if he does not issue orders, people will follow him. But if the ruler is corrupt, even if he repeatedly issues orders, people...
On Zi Lu 13.3	124	Without establishing proper titles, one's...
When in the Village 10.12	183	If the sitting mat is not laid according to the rituals, do...
When in the Village 10.26	186	Before boarding the carriage, stand upright and hold the carriage band for support to ascend. In the carriage, do not peer around, speak loudly or point with your finger.

Xue 学

Chapter	Pg no.	Translation
On Learning 1.1	30	Isn't it a joy to acquire knowledge and be...
On Governing 2.15	32	Reading and studying without thinking is...
On Transmitting 7.2	35	Remembering the knowledge I have learnt...
On Tai Bo 8.17	40	Study as if time is not on your side. Learn...
On Yang Huo 17.8	42	Those who love benevolence but not learning may be easily fooled; those who love knowledge but not learning may lack self-control; those who love honesty but not learning may be taken advantage of; those who love frankness but not learning may hurt others with their rashness; those who love courage but not learning may cause chaos; those who love staunchness but not learning may be brash and reckless.
On Zi Zhang 19.13	44	Leisure time from studying should be spent...
On Duke Ling of Wei 15.31	134	I once tried to go without food for the whole day, and without sleep for the whole night, to meditate and think; but it produced little results. I should have spent...
On Duke Ling of Wei 15.32	163	A gentleman seeks the Way above seeking food. In farming, we may sometimes go hungry; in learning, one may receive an official salary. A gentleman is concerned about the Way and not about poverty.
On Governing 2.4	166	At fifteen, I set my mind to acquire knowledge. At thirty, I establish my foundation. At forty, I learnt to manage perplexities. At fifty, I came to understand heaven's will for me. At sixty, I was able to decern the truth in others'...
Xian Questions 14.35	175	Even if no one understands me, I will not blame heaven or man, for I received my enlightenment by learning from everyday...
On Yang Huo 17.9	189	My students, why didn't you study the *Book of Songs*? The *Book of Songs* can stimulate your passions, enhance your cultural understanding, develop in you a heart for relations, and help you in expressing...

Xing 行

Chapter	Pg no.	Translation
On Transmitting 7.22	37	Whenever I travel with others, there is always something I can learn from them. By observing them, I would pick out the virtues to...
On Transmitting 7.24	47	Do you suspect that I am holding back some of my knowledge from you? There is nothing I keep from you. This is what I, Kong Qiu, am...
On Transmitting 7.25	48	Confucius educated his students in four...
On Duke Ling of Wei 15.24	64	Zi Gong asked: "Is there a single word that one can follow as a life principle?" Confucius: "Yes! It is perhaps 'consideration'. Do not do...
On Learning 1.11	67	When a man's father is alive, check his aspirations. When a man's father is deceased, observe his conduct. If he did not waver...
On Duke Ling of Wei 15.18	80	When one abides by righteousness as a principle of life, adheres to the rites, speaks with modesty and is trustworthy in all his...
On Gong Ye Zhang 5.7	83	If my way does not work, I will take a small...
On Duke Ling of Wei 15.17	113	Those who gather for small talk all day long without speaking of what is right or true, but only to display their petty cleverness...
On Virtue 4.12	114	He who acts only with a view to his own advantage...
On Governing 2.18	128	Listen more, reflect on what you hear, be careful with your speech; in this way, one will make less mistakes. Observe more, think...
On Virtue 4.24	129	A gentleman is slow to speak but prompt in action.
On Transmitting 7.33	131	In terms of knowledge, I am quite accomplished. But as to being a practising...
On Governing 2.22	137	If a person is not trustworthy, how can he establish himself? If a cart has no collar bar and a carriage has no yoke, how can...
On Gong Ye Zhang 5.10	150	...I used to believe that men practised what they said. But now, I will measure a...
On Duke Ling of Wei 15.25	155	...Men of three dynasties have done the same, and that has kept them on the right...

Reflections on the *Analects*

I read, I think and I write.

Confucius said, "We can gain new insights through reviewing old material."

What messages have you got
from reading the *Analects*?
Write down what you have learnt
to complete the learning experience.

Isn't it a joy to acquire knowledge and be able to put it to use?

Isn't it a great pleasure to have a friend visiting from afar?

If you understand, say that you understand. If you do not understand, say that you do not understand. That is true knowledge indeed!

Whenever I travel with others, there is always something I can learn from them.

A simple bowl of rice, a plain cup of water, living in a shabby hut—most men would not be able to withstand such misery, but Yan Hui manages to remain so joyful.

Having a simple meal, propping up on my arms for a nap, joy can be found in such.

Ill-gotten riches are to me just as clouds passing in the sky.

Only in winter can one see that the cypress and the pine are the last to shed their leaves.

The army may lose its commander, but a man cannot lose his aspirations.

If I hear and grasp the truth in the morning, and die in the evening, I will have no regrets.

论语的启示

孔子的智慧真谛

绘画 ：萧承财

翻译 ：杨立平

亚太图书有限公司出版